The New Air Fryer

Cookbook for Beginners UK

1900 Days Easy and EffortlessAir Fryer Recipes for Beginners
and Busy People to Cook Faster and Healthier

Greg I. Moran

Contents

Introduction *1*

Getting to Know Your Air Fryer 1

Foods to Cook in Air Fryer and Foods to Avoid
.... 2

Benefits of an Air Fryer 3

Possible Risks 5

How to Clean Your Air Fryer 6

Tips and Tricks for Your Air Fryer 7

Chapter 1: Breakfast *8*

Shakshuka 8

Banana bread French toast 8

Air Fryer Breakfast Pockets 8

Air Fryer Breakfast Quinoa Bowls 9

Croque madame 9

Huevos rancheros 9

Chorizo and egg breakfast skillet 10

Sausage and egg muffins....................... 10

Mushroom and spinach frittata 10

Blueberry pancakes.............................. 11

Smoked salmon and avocado toast 11

Welsh rarebit 11

Oatmeal breakfast bars 12

Breakfast egg rolls 12

Bubble and squeak patties 13

Sweet Potato and Black Bean Enchiladas ... 13

Air-fried Breakfast Sandwich with Sausage,
Egg, and Cheese 14

Air-fried Cinnamon Rolls 14

Air-fried Welsh Rarebit 14

Air Fried Bubble and Squeak.................. 14

Air Fried Breakfast Casserole.................. 15

Air Fried Kedgeree 15

Bacon Muffin Sandwiches 16

Air Fryer Pancakes With Blueberries 16

Cheesy Cauliflower "Hash Browns" 16

Chapter 2: BBQ *17*

Korean-style short ribs 17

Grilled octopus 17

Air Fryer BBQ Pulled Chicken 17

Spicy lamb skewers.............................. 18

Grilled oysters.................................... 18

Smoky pork shoulder 18

Tandoori chicken................................. 19

Moroccan-style grilled vegetables 19

Grilled prawns with garlic and lemon........ 19

Charred halloumi skewers 20

Jerk chicken wings 20

Grilled salmon with herb butter 20

BBQ beef brisket................................. 21

Grilled peaches with vanilla ice cream 21

Chapter 3: Family Favourites *22*

Turkey and stuffing meatballs................. 22

Cheese and onion pasties 22

Air fryer garlic shrimp 22

Air fryer shepherd's pie 23

Cauliflower mac and cheese bites 23

Stuffed peppers 23

Air fryer falafel 24

Air fryer chicken and waffles 24

Buffalo chicken strips 25

Air fryer pizza.................................... 25

Air fryer sweet potato fries 25

Air fryer quiche 26

Air fryer cornbread 26

Chicken curry 26

Air Fryer Fruit and Pork Kebabs 27

Shepherd's pie 27

Air Fryer Peach and Blueberry Crumble ... 28

Radish Chips 28

Air Fryer Apple Cinnamon French Toast ... 29

Bangers and mash 29

Steak and Kidney Pie 29

Vegetarian shepherd's pie with lentils 30

Spaghetti Zoodles and Meatballs 31

Turkey Mince Pasta Bake 31

Chapter 4: Poultry 32

Chicken and Mushroom Pie 32

Chicken Breasts with Asparagus and Beans 32

Jerk chicken 33

Lemon herb turkey breast 33

Duck spring rolls.............................. 33

Pesto chicken thighs 34

Curry chicken wings 34

Honey mustard duck breast.................. 34

Spicy chicken skewers 35

Cajun turkey burgers 35

Lemon garlic chicken kabobs 35

Jamaican-style curry turkey legs.............. 36

Peri peri chicken thighs 36

Cranberry stuffed turkey meatloaf 36

Lemon-Pepper Chicken Drumsticks 37

Chicken and Vegetable Curry 37

Peanut Butter Chicken Salad 38

Air Fryer Stuffed Chicken Breast with Spinach and Feta 38

Tandoori Chicken 38

20 Chicken Croquettes with Creole Sauce ... 39

Nacho Chicken Fries 39

Air Fried Chicken Wings with BBQ Sauce 40

Chapter 5: Fish and Seafood............ 41

Air fryer blackened salmon................... 41

Spicy shrimp skewers 41

Crispy fried squid rings 41

Seafood stuffed mushrooms 42

Scallop and bacon bites 42

Teriyaki glazed salmon skewers 42

Coconut shrimp 43

Grilled sardines 43

Cajun-style tilapia 43

Crab cakes 44

Lemon garlic shrimp and asparagus 44

Tandoori salmon 44

Cajun shrimp and grits 45

Pesto crusted sea bass 45

Miso glazed cod 45

COD TRAYBAKE 46

Air Fryer Garlic Butter Shrimp Scampi 46

Tuna with Roasted Garlic and Hazelnuts ... 47

Stuffed Sole Florentine 47

20 FISH KEBABS 47

Smoky Prawns and Chorizo Tapas 48

Air Fryer Cajun Shrimp Po' Boys 48

Cod Tacos with Mango Salsa 49

Air Fried Shrimp Skewers with Lemon Garlic Butter 49

Chapter 6: Beef, Pork, and Lamb 50

Roast beef and Yorkshire Pudding 50

Korean-style beef skewers 50

Jamaican jerk pork chops 51

Mexican-style beef empanadas 51

Chinese-style beef and broccoli 52

Moroccan spiced lamb chops 52

Stuffed pork tenderloin 52

Indian-spiced beef burgers 53

Mexican-style pork carnitas 53

Greek lamb meatballs 54

Caribbean-style beef brisket 54

Vietnamese-style pork chops 54

Moroccan-style beef skewers 55

French-style lamb chops with dijon mustard 55

Thai-style pork stir-fry 55

Jamaican-style oxtail stew 56

Italian-style meatball sub 56

Reuben Beef Rolls with Thousand Island
Sauce 57

French Dip Sandwich 57

Air Fried Crispy Venison 58

20 Pork Schnitzels with Sour Cream and Dill
Sauce 58

Herb-Crusted Lamb Chops 59

Sichuan Cumin Lamb 59

Chapter 7: Snacks and Appetisers 60

Thai-style shrimp cakes 60

Indian-style samosas 60

Italian-style arancini balls 61

Chinese-style pork dumplings................. 61

Mexican-style churros........................ 62

Greek-style spanakopita 62

Japanese-style takoyaki 63

Jamaican-style plantain chips 63

Spanish-style croquetas 63

Cajun-style popcorn shrimp 64

Italian-style pizza rolls 64

Lebanese-style kibbeh balls 64

Moroccan-style vegetable pastries 65

Filipino-style lumpia 65

Air Fryer Ranch Seasoned Pretzel Bites...... 66

Shishito Peppers with Herb Dressing 66

Lemony Pear Chips........................... 67

Air Fryer Hashbrowns Recipe 67

20 Crispy Mozzarella Sticks 67

Chilli-Brined Fried Calamari 68

Crispy Breaded Beef Cubes 68

Chapter 8:Healthy Vegetarian and vegan Recipes 69

Crispy zucchini fries 69

Indian-style vegetable pakoras 69

Spicy cauliflower bites 69

Korean-style tofu bowls 70

Greek-style stuffed peppers.................... 70

Middle Eastern-style falafel burgers 71

Italian-style eggplant parmesan 71

Jamaican-style jerk tofu 72

Thai-style tofu satay 72

Lebanese-style falafel wraps 72

Italian-style warm caprese salad 73

Mexican-style black bean taquitos 73

Chinese-style vegetable dumplings........... 74

Mediterranean-style stuffed artichokes 74

Indian-style samosa chaat 75

Italian-style stuffed mushrooms 75

Korean-style tofu lettuce wraps 75

Middle Eastern-style stuffed grape leaves ... 76

Lentil Soup 76

20 Air Fryer Tofu Stir Fry with Vegetables... 77

Tofu Wrap 77

Vegan Roasted Vegetable Quinoa Bowl 77

Salmon with Roasted Vegetables 78

Vegan Stuffed Bell Peppers..................... 78

Air Fried Vegetable Fajitas with Guacamole 79

Air Fried Stuffed Portobello Mushrooms ... 79

Chapter 9:Desserts 80

Glazed donuts 80

Lava cake with vanilla ice cream 80

Mini Peanut Butter Tarts 81

Apple Pie 81

Quiche Lorraine 82

Rich chocolatey custard 82

Chocolate Cheesecake 83

Air fryer Olives 83

Grilled Air Fryer Peaches: 83

10 Air fryer Banana Souffle 83

Mixed Berries with Pecan Streusel Topping 84

Pumpkin Pudding with Vanilla Wafers 84

Blackberry Peach Cobbler with Vanilla 84

Air fryer Yorkshire pudding 85

Air fryer Apple fries 85

Air Fryer Coconut Shrimp with Sweet Chilli

Sauce 85

Air Fryer Carrot Fries with Honey Mustard Dip

.... 86

Grilled Pineapple Dessert 86

Introduction

Hello, and welcome to my Air Fryer Cookbook for Beginners. I'm thrilled to be sharing my love for cooking with you through this book, and I hope that it inspires you to explore the many possibilities that air frying has to offer.

I grew up in a family where food was at the centre of everything. My mother was an incredible cook who always made sure we had delicious, homemade meals on the table. As a child, I loved helping her in the kitchen, and as I grew older, my love for cooking and experimenting with new recipes only grew stronger.

Over the years, I have tried many different cooking techniques, but when I discovered air frying, it completely changed the game for me. I was blown away by how easy it was to create crispy, delicious meals without all the excess oil and grease that comes with traditional frying methods. I quickly fell in love with my air fryer and started experimenting with all sorts of different recipes.

Now, as someone who has been using an air fryer for years, I am excited to share my knowledge and experience with others who are just starting out. I understand how intimidating it can be to try out new kitchen tools and techniques, especially if you are not an experienced cook. That's why I want to create an approachable and user-friendly cookbook that will help beginners feel confident and inspired to get cooking with their air fryer.

When I first started using an air fryer, I was a little intimidated by the machine and wasn't quite sure what to make with it. But with a little experimentation and some help from online resources, I quickly fell in love with the convenience and versatility of air frying. It's become my go-to method for cooking up delicious, healthy meals in a flash.

In this cookbook, I'll be sharing some of my favourite air fryer recipes that are perfect for beginners. Each recipe has been tested and refined to make sure it's easy to follow and turns out perfectly every time. Whether you're looking for a quick and easy breakfast, a hearty dinner, or a sweet treat, you'll find something in this cookbook to suit your taste.

But this cookbook isn't just about recipes. I also want to share some tips and tricks for getting the most out of your air fryer. From choosing the right ingredients to using the right cooking times and temperatures, I'll walk you through everything you need to know to become an air fryer pro.

Finally, I want to encourage you to have fun with your air fryer. Cooking should be an enjoyable experience, and the air fryer makes it easy to whip up delicious meals with minimal effort. Don't be afraid to experiment and try new things – you never know what culinary delights you might discover!

So, let's get started on this culinary adventure together. I can't wait to see what amazing meals you'll create with your air fryer. Happy cooking!

Getting to Know Your Air Fryer

As a beginner in the world of air frying, it's important to understand what an air fryer is and why it's worth adding to your kitchen. Simply put, an air fryer is a compact kitchen appliance that uses hot air to cook food, allowing you to achieve crispy and golden results without the need for deep frying.

The hot air circulates rapidly around the food, creating a crispy exterior without the need for excess oil. This means that you can enjoy your favourite fried foods with less guilt, as they are significantly healthier than traditional deep-fried foods. In addition to frying, air fryers can also bake, grill, and roast, making them incredibly versatile appliances for any kitchen. With their ease of use, quick cooking times, and healthier cooking methods, air fryers have become increasingly popular in recent years, and for good reason!

But the benefits of an air fryer go beyond just healthier cooking. It's also incredibly versatile and can be used to cook a wide range of foods, from chicken wings to vegetables and even desserts. And because it uses hot air to cook, you can expect your food to be cooked evenly and quickly, without the need for waiting for the oil to heat up.

Another advantage of an air fryer is its convenience. It's a great tool for busy people who want to prepare meals quickly and easily. Many air fryer recipes require only a few simple ingredients, and the cooking time is often shorter than traditional cooking methods. Plus, cleanup is a breeze, with most air fryer baskets and accessories being dishwasher-safe.

When it comes to choosing an air fryer, there are a few factors to consider. Size is important, as you'll want to choose a model that fits your needs and your kitchen space. If you're cooking for one or two people, a smaller air fryer might be sufficient, while larger families may want a bigger model.

You'll also want to consider the features that come with the air fryer. Some models have presets for specific types of food, like chicken or fish, while others have the ability to bake or roast as well. And if you're short on kitchen space, there are even compact air fryer models that can be easily stored away when not in use.

In summary, an air fryer is a valuable addition to any kitchen, providing healthier, versatile, and convenient cooking options. As you begin your air frying journey, don't be afraid to experiment with different recipes and techniques to find what works best for you. With a little practice and creativity, you'll be whipping up delicious and healthy meals in no time.

Foods to Cook in Air Fryer and Foods to Avoid

Cooking with an air fryer is a fun and exciting experience that opens up a whole new world of culinary possibilities. With this amazing appliance, you can cook a wide variety of foods to crispy perfection, without the need for excess oil or deep frying. However, while the air fryer can cook many foods to perfection, there are some foods that are not well-suited for this cooking method.

Let's start with the good news – there are many types of food that are perfect for cooking in an air fryer. Some of our favourites include:

- Chicken wings: Air-fried chicken wings are crispy, juicy, and downright delicious. Simply toss them in your favourite seasoning or sauce and let the air fryer work its magic.
- French fries: Say goodbye to greasy fast-food fries and hello to crispy, perfectly cooked fries made in the air fryer. They are healthier, tastier, and super easy to make.
- Fish: Whether you are cooking salmon, cod, or any other type of fish, the air fryer is a great way to get perfectly crispy skin and tender, flaky flesh.
- Vegetables: From brussels sprouts to carrots to asparagus, the air fryer can turn any veggie into a crispy, delicious side dish.
- Baked goods: Yes, you can even bake in the air fryer! Think muffins, cupcakes, and even small cakes.
- Pork chops and pork tenderloin: The air fryer is perfect for cooking juicy

pork chops and tenderloin with a crispy exterior.

- Hamburgers and sliders: Cooking burgers in the air fryer gives them a delicious crispy crust while keeping them moist and juicy on the inside.
- Meatballs: Air frying meatballs creates a crispy exterior while keeping them tender and juicy on the inside.
- Falafel: The air fryer is perfect for cooking crispy falafel without the need for deep frying.
- Spring rolls: Air frying spring rolls creates a crispy texture without the added oil of deep frying.
- Mozzarella sticks: The air fryer creates perfectly crispy and melty mozzarella sticks without the need for a deep fryer.
- Chicken nuggets or tenders: Air frying chicken nuggets or tenders creates a crispy coating while keeping the inside moist and tender.
- Onion rings: Air frying onion rings creates a delicious crispy texture without the need for a lot of oil.
- Corn on the cob: The air fryer is perfect for roasting corn on the cob, giving it a delicious roasted flavor and crispy texture.
- Baked potatoes: The air fryer can cook baked potatoes in half the time it takes in the oven, with a crispy skin and fluffy interior.
- Grilled cheese sandwiches: The air fryer can make grilled cheese sandwiches with a perfectly crispy exterior and gooey melted cheese inside.
- Churros or donuts: Air frying churros or donuts creates a crispy exterior while keeping the inside soft and fluffy.

Now, let's talk about the foods that are not well-suited for cooking in an air fryer. These include:

- Foods with wet batters: Foods that are heavily battered or coated in wet ingredients like batter or breadcrumbs don't fare well in the air fryer. They tend to come out soggy and unappetizing.
- Delicate foods: Foods like flaky fish or delicate pastries may not hold up well in the air fryer and could easily fall apart.
- Liquid-heavy foods: Foods like stews or soups are not suitable for the air fryer. They require a moist cooking environment, which the air fryer cannot provide.
- Large cuts of meat: While the air fryer is great for smaller cuts of meat like chicken breasts or pork chops, it's not ideal for larger cuts like a whole chicken or roast.\

Overall, the air fryer is a versatile and convenient appliance that can cook many types of food to perfection. Just remember to avoid wet batters, delicate foods, liquid-heavy dishes, and larger cuts of meat, and you'll be well on your way to air-fried success.

Benefits of an Air Fryer

Air fryers have gained immense popularity in recent years due to their unique cooking method that uses hot air to fry food, resulting in healthier and more delicious meals. In this section, we will discuss the top benefits of owning an air fryer.

Healthier Meals: Air fryers offer a healthier alternative to traditional deep frying methods, as they use only a small amount of oil to cook food. This means that meals cooked in an air fryer have significantly less fat and calories compared to those that are deep-fried, making them a healthier option for those looking to maintain a balanced diet.

Additionally, air frying helps to reduce the formation of harmful chemicals such as acrylamide that can occur when cooking certain foods at high temperatures. Acrylamide is a chemical that can form in starchy foods such as potatoes, when they are cooked at high temperatures, such as when deep-fried. Air fryers use less oil and cook food at a lower temperature, which reduces the risk of acrylamide formation.

Convenience: Cooking with an air fryer is incredibly easy and convenient. With just a few buttons, you can set the temperature and time and let the air fryer do the rest.

Another benefit of using an air fryer is its quick cooking time. Compared to traditional ovens or stovetops, air fryers cook food much faster, which is great for those who are short on time. This also means that the air fryer uses less energy, making it an eco-friendly option.

Versatility: Air fryers can cook a wide variety of foods, from chicken wings to roasted vegetables, making them a versatile kitchen tool. You can even bake cakes and bread in some models.

Saves Time: Air fryers use a powerful fan to circulate hot air around the food, resulting in faster and more even cooking. This means that you can cook meals in less time than traditional methods such as baking, roasting, or deep-frying. For example, you can cook a batch of chicken wings in just 15 minutes, compared to 30-45 minutes in an oven. This time-saving feature makes air fryers a great option for busy individuals or families who want to enjoy a healthy and delicious meal without sacrificing their valuable time.

Easy to Clean: Cleaning an air fryer is much easier than traditional frying pans or ovens. Most air fryer models come with removable parts that can be easily taken apart and cleaned. These parts can be washed in the dishwasher, saving you time and effort in cleaning up after cooking. Plus, the air fryer's compact size means it doesn't take up much counter space, and you won't have to deal with the hassle of cleaning a large oven or stove. With the convenience of easy cleaning, you can spend more time enjoying your delicious, healthy meals and less time worrying about the mess.

Energy Efficient: Using an air fryer to cook your meals can significantly reduce your energy consumption, as they require less time and lower temperatures to cook food compared to traditional ovens. This means that you can save money on your electricity bills while also reducing your impact on the environment. Additionally, air fryers are often smaller than

ovens, which means that they take up less space and use less energy to heat up. Choosing to use an air fryer instead of a traditional oven can be a simple yet effective way to live a more sustainable lifestyle.

No Unpleasant Odours: Traditional frying methods can leave an unpleasant smell in your kitchen, but air fryers don't. The hot air circulates inside the fryer, which means there's no oil or grease splattering, resulting in a clean and odourless kitchen.

Safe to Use: Air fryers are generally safe to use, with most models having safety features such as automatic shut-off and cool-touch handles. This makes them a great option for families with children or anyone concerned about kitchen safety.

In conclusion, owning an air fryer has numerous benefits, from healthier meals to convenience and versatility. It's a worthwhile investment for anyone who loves delicious and healthy food without the hassle of traditional cooking methods.

Possible Risks

While air fryers offer many benefits, it's important to note that there are also some potential risks associated with using them. Here are a few risks to consider:

- Burns: The air fryer heats up to high temperatures, and the basket can get very hot. If not used carefully, this can result in burns. It's important to use oven mitts or tongs when removing the basket from the fryer and to keep the fryer away from children and pets.
- Overcooking: It's easy to overcook food in an air fryer, especially if you're not familiar with the cooking times and temperatures. Overcooked food can be dry and unappetizing, so it's important to follow the instructions carefully and keep an eye on your food as it cooks.
- Air quality: When cooking with an air fryer, the hot air can release fumes and particles into the air. This can be a concern for individuals with respiratory issues, allergies, or asthma. It's important to use the air fryer in a well-ventilated area to minimise the risk of inhaling these particles.
- Maintenance: Air fryers require regular maintenance to function properly. This includes cleaning the basket and removing any grease or food particles that may have accumulated. If not cleaned regularly, the air fryer can become a breeding ground for bacteria and other harmful microorganisms.
- Non-stick coating: Many air fryer baskets have a non-stick coating that can wear off over time. If ingested, this coating can be harmful to your health. It's important to inspect the basket regularly and replace it if you notice any signs of wear and tear.

While these risks should be considered, they can be mitigated by following the instructions carefully, using the air fryer in a well-ventilated area, and performing regular maintenance. With proper use and care, an air fryer can be a safe and convenient addition to your kitchen.

How to Clean Your Air Fryer

Cleaning your air fryer is important to keep it in good working condition and to ensure that your food stays healthy and free from contamination. Here are 8 steps to clean your air fryer:

- Unplug the air fryer: Before cleaning your air fryer, ensure it's unplugged and has cooled down completely.
- Remove the basket: Take out the frying basket and detach any removable components like the cooking tray, racks, and separator. Some air fryers may have dishwasher-safe components, so check your manual to confirm which parts are dishwasher safe.
- Soak the basket: If your air fryer has a non-stick coating, you can soak the basket in warm, soapy water for 10-15 minutes. This will help loosen any food particles stuck to the basket.
- Clean the basket: After soaking, use a non-abrasive sponge or cloth to scrub the basket gently. Don't use abrasive scrubbers or steel wool pads as they can scratch the non-stick coating.
- Clean the interior: Use a damp cloth or sponge to wipe the interior of the air fryer. Don't use any abrasive cleaners or scouring pads as they can scratch the surface.
- Clean the heating element: If there's any food residue on the heating element, use a soft-bristled brush to clean it. Be gentle to avoid damaging the heating element.
- Clean the exterior: Wipe the exterior of the air fryer with a damp cloth or sponge. Don't use any harsh cleaning products or abrasive materials.
- Dry the components: After cleaning, dry all the components thoroughly before reassembling the air fryer. You can use a clean towel or air-dry the components.

Remember, always refer to your air fryer's manual for specific cleaning instructions, especially if it has non-removable parts or components that require special cleaning.

By following these simple steps, you can keep your air fryer in top condition and ensure that it continues to provide you with delicious and healthy meals for years to come.

Here are some things to check for when cleaning your air fryer:

- Examine the interior of the air fryer for any food residue or oil buildup that may have accumulated during cooking.
- Check the heating element for any food debris or oil that may have splattered onto it.
- Make sure to clean the air fryer basket thoroughly, especially around the edges and corners where food may get stuck.
- Check the air intake vents to make sure they are not clogged with food debris, which can cause the air fryer to malfunction.
- Make sure the heating element is completely dry before using the air fryer again to prevent electrical shock.
- Check the power cord and plug for any damage, and ensure they are completely dry before using the air fryer again.

- Check the air fryer's instruction manual for any specific cleaning instructions or warnings.

Tips and Tricks for Your Air Fryer

Congratulations on getting your new air fryer! Cooking with an air fryer is a fun and healthy way to prepare your meals. However, like any new kitchen gadget, there's a bit of a learning curve. Here are some tips and tricks to help you get the most out of your air fryer:

- Preheat the Air Fryer: Just like with any other cooking method, preheating your air fryer can make a big difference in the outcome of your food. It can help ensure that your food cooks evenly and reduces the overall cooking time.
- Shake the Basket: To ensure that your food is cooked evenly, it's a good idea to shake the basket or toss the food halfway through the cooking process. This will help ensure that all sides of the food are evenly browned.
- Use Accessories: Many air fryers come with accessories such as baking pans or skewers. Experiment with these accessories to cook a wider variety of foods.
- Use Parchment Paper: If you're worried about your food sticking to the air fryer basket, you can use parchment paper. Simply cut a piece of parchment paper to fit the basket and place your food on top. This will help prevent your food from sticking and make cleanup easier.
- Use Cooking Spray: Another way to prevent your food from sticking is to use cooking spray. Simply spray the air fryer basket with cooking spray before adding your food.
- Don't Overcrowd the Basket: It's important not to overcrowd the air fryer basket, as this can prevent your food from cooking evenly. Instead, cook in batches and make sure that there's enough space between each piece of food.
- Experiment with Seasonings: One of the best things about cooking with an air fryer is that it's easy to experiment with different seasonings and flavourings. Try using different spices, herbs, or marinades to add flavour to your food.
- Season Food Before Cooking: Add seasoning to your food before cooking to infuse it with flavour and ensure that the seasoning adheres to the food.
- Experiment with Different Foods: The air fryer can cook a variety of foods beyond just chicken and fries. Try cooking vegetables, seafood, and even desserts!
- Let the Food Rest: Just like with any other cooking method, it's important to let your food rest for a few minutes before serving. This will help ensure that the juices redistribute and the food stays moist.
- Clean the Air Fryer Regularly: To ensure that your air fryer lasts as long as possible, it's important to clean it regularly. Make sure to remove any food particles or grease from the basket and wipe down the exterior with a damp cloth.
- Use a Meat Thermometer: Use a meat thermometer to ensure that your meat is cooked to the appropriate temperature, as cooking times can vary depending on the size and thickness of the meat.

With these tips and tricks, you'll be able to make the most out of your air fryer and create delicious and healthy meals with ease.

Chapter 1: Breakfast

Shakshuka

Serves: 2

Prep time: 10 minutes / Cook time: 20 minutes

Ingredients:

- 1 tablespoon olive oil
- 1/2 onion, chopped
- 1/2 red pepper, chopped
- 1 garlic clove, minced
- 1 teaspoon paprika
- 1/2 teaspoon cumin
- 1/4 teaspoon cayenne pepper
- 1 can (14 oz) diced tomatoes
- Salt and pepper to taste
- 4 eggs
- Fresh parsley or cilantro, chopped for garnish

Instructions:

1. Preheat the air fryer to 180°C.
2. In a skillet, heat the olive oil over medium heat.
3. Add the onion and red pepper, and sauté until the onion is translucent.
4. Add the garlic, paprika, cumin, and cayenne pepper, and cook for another minute.
5. Add the diced tomatoes and season with salt and pepper to taste. Cook for 5-7 minutes until the sauce is slightly thickened.
6. Carefully transfer the tomato sauce to an oven-safe dish that fits in the air fryer.
7. Use a spoon to create 4 wells in the tomato sauce.
8. Crack an egg into each well.
9. Fry for 8-10 minutes. Fry until the egg whites are set but the yolks are still runny.
10. Garnish with fresh parsley or cilantro, and serve immediately with crusty bread.

Banana bread French toast

Serves: 2-4

Prep time: 10 minutes / Cook time: 10 minutes

Ingredients:

- 4 slices of day-old banana bread
- 2 eggs
- 60ml milk
- 1/2 teaspoon vanilla extract
- 1/2 teaspoon cinnamon
- 15g butter
- Maple syrup and sliced bananas for serving

Instructions:

1. Preheat the air fryer to 180°C.
2. Cut the banana bread into 1-inch thick slices.
3. In a shallow bowl, whisk together the eggs, milk, vanilla extract, and cinnamon.
4. Dip each slice of banana bread into the egg mixture, making sure both sides are coated.
5. Melt the butter in a skillet over medium heat.
6. Add the banana bread slices to the skillet and cook for 2-3 minutes on each side until golden brown.
7. Transfer the cooked French toast to the air fryer basket.
8. Fry for 2-4 minutes..
9. Serve with maple syrup and sliced bananas.

Air Fryer Breakfast Pockets

Serves: 4

Prep time: 10 minutes / Cook time: 10 minutes

Ingredients:

- 1 sheet puff pastry, thawed
- 4 slices of ham
- 4 slices of cheddar cheese
- 4 eggs
- Salt and pepper to taste
- 1 tablespoon chopped chives

Instructions:

1. Preheat the air fryer to 180°C.
2. Cut the puff pastry sheet into 4 equal squares.
3. Place a slice of ham and a slice of cheddar cheese on one half of each square.
4. Crack an egg on top of the ham and cheese.
5. Season with salt and pepper, and sprinkle with chopped chives.
6. Fold the other half of the puff pastry square over

the filling and press the edges together to seal.

7. Place the breakfast pockets in the air fryer basket.
8. Fry for 8-10 minutes.
9. Serve and enjoy!

Air Fryer Breakfast Quinoa Bowls

Serves: 4

Prep time: 10 minutes / Cook time: 32 minutes

Ingredients:

- 250g quinoa
- 240ml water
- 1/4 tsp salt
- 1/4 tsp black pepper
- 120g canned black beans, drained and rinsed
- 1/2 avocado, diced
- 60ml chopped fresh cilantro
- 2 large eggs
- 15ml olive oil
- Salsa (optional)

Instructions:

1. Rinse the quinoa in a fine-mesh sieve under running water until the water runs clear.
2. In a medium saucepan, bring the quinoa, water, salt, and black pepper to a boil over medium-high heat.
3. Reduce the heat to low, cover the pot, and simmer until the quinoa is tender and the water has been absorbed, about 15 minutes.
4. Remove the pot from the heat and let it sit covered for 5 minutes.
5. In a large skillet, heat the olive oil over medium heat.
6. Add the black beans and cook for 1-2 minutes until heated through.
7. Add the cooked quinoa and stir to combine with the beans.
8. Place Ingredients into the air fryer basket.
9. Crack the eggs into the basket on top of the quinoa and beans.
10. Cook until the eggs are set, about 4-5 minutes.
11. Top with diced avocado and chopped cilantro.
12. Serve with salsa, if desired.

Croque madame

Serves: 2

Prep time: 10 minutes / Cook time: 12 minutes

Ingredients:

- 4 slices of bread
- 2 tbsp unsalted butter
- 1 tbsp all-purpose flour
- 120ml cup whole milk
- 1/4 tsp ground nutmeg
- Sea salt and ground black pepper, to taste
- 1/2 cup grated Gruyere cheese
- 2 thin slices of cooked ham
- 2 large eggs

Instructions:

1. In a small saucepan, melt 1 tbsp of butter over medium heat. Add the flour and whisk for 1 minute until well combined.
2. Gradually add the milk while whisking constantly to avoid lumps.
3. Add the nutmeg, salt, and pepper, and whisk until the mixture thickens, for about 5 minutes. Remove from heat and stir in the grated cheese. Set the cheese sauce aside.
4. Lay the bread slices on a clean surface and spread 1 tbsp of butter on one side of each slice.
5. Place a slice of ham on two of the bread slices, and spread the cheese sauce on top of the ham.
6. Place the remaining bread slices on top of the cheese sauce, butter side up.
7. Preheat the air fryer to 180°C. Place the sandwiches on the crisper plate and air fry for 6 minutes.
8. Remove the crisper plate and make a small well in the centre of each sandwich. Crack an egg into each well and return the crisper plate to the air fryer. Air fry for another 6 minutes or until the egg whites are set but the yolks are still runny.
9. Serve immediately.

Huevos rancheros

Serves: 2

Prep time: 10 minutes / Cook time: 15 minutes

Ingredients:

- 4 corn tortillas
- 4 large eggs
- 120g canned black beans, drained and rinsed
- 120g salsa
- 120g crumbled feta cheese
- 60g chopped fresh cilantro

- 1 small avocado, sliced
- Sea salt and ground black pepper, to taste

Instructions:

1. Preheat the air fryer to 180°C.
2. Place the corn tortillas on the crisper plate and air fry for 5 minutes, or until crispy.
3. In a small bowl, whisk the eggs with salt and pepper.
4. Place the black beans in a small microwave-safe bowl and microwave for 30 seconds or until heated through.
5. Spread the salsa on top of each tortilla, leaving a well in the centre. Pour the eggs into the well, and top with the heated black beans and crumbled feta cheese.
6. Return the crisper plate to the air fryer and air fry for another 8-10 minutes, or until the eggs are cooked to your liking.
7. Remove the crisper plate from the air fryer and sprinkle the chopped cilantro on top of the eggs.
8. Serve with sliced avocado on the side.

Chorizo and egg breakfast skillet

Serves: 2

Prep time: 10 minutes / Cook time: 15 minutes

Ingredients:

- 113g chorizo sausage, sliced
- 150g diced onion
- 150g diced pepper
- 1 small garlic clove, minced
- 4 large eggs
- 60g shredded cheddar cheese
- 1 tbsp chopped fresh parsley
- Sea salt and ground black pepper, to taste

Instructions:

1. Preheat the air fryer to 180°C.
2. Add the sliced chorizo to the crisper basket and air fry for 3-4 minutes, or until browned.
3. Add the diced onion, pepper, and garlic to the crisper basket, and air fry for another 5-6 minutes, or until the vegetables are soft and lightly browned.
4. Whisk the eggs in a small bowl and season with salt and pepper to taste.
5. Pour the egg mixture into the crisper basket and

sprinkle with shredded cheddar cheese. Air fry for 5-6 minutes, or until the eggs are set and the cheese is melted and bubbly.
6. Sprinkle with chopped fresh parsley and serve hot.
7. This chorizo and egg breakfast skillet is perfect for a hearty and delicious breakfast or brunch. Enjoy!

Sausage and egg muffins

Serves: 2

Prep time: 5 minutes / Cook time: 10 minutes

Ingredients:

- 2 English muffins, split
- 4 pork sausages (200g)
- 2 large eggs
- 20g cheddar cheese, grated
- 1 tsp olive oil
- Sea salt and ground black pepper, to taste

Instructions:

1. Preheat the air fryer to 180°C.
2. Arrange the sausages on the crisper plate and brush them with 1 teaspoon of olive oil.
3. Air fry for 7 minutes or until fully cooked, turning them over halfway through cooking.
4. Remove the sausages from the air fryer and slice them lengthwise.
5. Arrange the English muffins on the crisper plate and air fry for 2 minutes or until lightly toasted.
6. Remove the muffins from the air fryer and top each half with a slice of sausage and grated cheddar cheese.
7. Crack an egg into each well of a silicone muffin cup.
8. Season the eggs with salt and pepper.
9. Place the muffin cups on the crisper plate and air fry for 5 minutes or until the eggs are cooked to your liking.
10. Serve the eggs on top of the sausage and cheese-topped English muffins. Enjoy!

Mushroom and spinach frittata

Serves: 2

Prep time: 10 minutes / Cook time: 20 minutes

Ingredients:

- 4 large eggs
- 60g button mushrooms, sliced
- 30g baby spinach leaves
- 20g cheddar cheese, grated
- 1 garlic clove, minced
- 1 tsp olive oil
- Sea salt and ground black pepper, to taste

Instructions:

1. Preheat the air fryer to 180°C.
2. In a bowl, whisk the eggs and season with salt and pepper.
3. In a small frying pan, heat 1 teaspoon of olive oil over medium heat.
4. Add the mushrooms and garlic, and sauté for 3 minutes or until the mushrooms are tender.
5. Add the baby spinach leaves to the frying pan and sauté for 1 minute or until wilted.
6. Pour the egg mixture into the frying pan and sprinkle with grated cheddar cheese.
7. Place the frying pan on the crisper plate and air fry for 15 minutes or until the frittata is set and the cheese is melted and bubbly. Remove the frying pan from the air fryer and let the frittata cool for a few minutes before slicing and serving. Enjoy!

Blueberry pancakes

Serves: 2

Prep time: 10 minutes / Cook time: 15 minutes

Ingredients:

- 80g plain flour
- 1 tbsp sugar
- 80 ml whole milk
- 40g blueberries
- Maple syrup and extra blueberries, to serve
- Sea salt, to taste
- 1 tsp baking powder
- 1 small egg, beaten
- 1 tsp vanilla extract
- 2 tsp butter, melted

Instructions:

1. Preheat the air fryer to 180°C.
2. In a mixing bowl, whisk together the flour, baking powder, sugar, and salt.
3. In a separate bowl, whisk together the egg, milk, and vanilla extract.

4. Pour the wet Ingredients into the dry Ingredients and stir until just combined. Fold in the blueberries.
5. Brush the air fryer basket with melted butter.
6. Drop the batter by spoonfuls into the air fryer basket, making 4 pancakes. Air fry the pancakes for 7-8 minutes or until golden brown and cooked through, flipping them over halfway through cooking.
7. Serve the pancakes with maple syrup and extra blueberries. Enjoy!

Smoked salmon and avocado toast

Serves: 2

Prep time: 10 minutes / Cook time: 5 minutes

Ingredients:

- 2 slices of whole-grain bread
- 1 ripe avocado, peeled, pitted, and mashed
- Juice of 1/2 lemon
- Sea salt and ground black pepper, to taste
- 113g smoked salmon
- 1 tbsp chopped fresh chives

Instructions:

1. Preheat the air fryer to 180°C.
2. Place the bread slices in the crisper basket and air fry for 3-4 minutes, or until toasted.
3. In a small bowl, mix the mashed avocado with the lemon juice, salt, and pepper.
4. Divide the avocado mixture between the two slices of toast, spreading it evenly.
5. Top each slice of toast with smoked salmon and sprinkle with chopped chives.
6. Serve immediately.

Welsh rarebit

Serves: 2

Prep time: 5 minutes / Cook time: 8 minutes

Ingredients:

- 2 slices of thick bread, such as sourdough or rye
- 1 tbsp unsalted butter
- 1 tbsp plain flour

- 120ml beer
- 1 tsp Dijon mustard
- 1 tsp Worcestershire sauce
- 1/2 tsp smoked paprika
- 120g grated cheddar cheese
- Sea salt and ground black pepper, to taste

Instructions:

1. Preheat the air fryer to 180°C.
2. Place the bread slices in the crisper basket and air fry for 3-4 minutes, or until toasted.
3. In a small saucepan, melt the butter over medium heat.
4. Whisk in the flour and cook for 1-2 minutes, or until the mixture turns a light brown colour.
5. Slowly whisk in the beer, mustard, Worcestershire sauce, and smoked paprika.
6. Continue cooking, whisking constantly, until the mixture thickens, about 3-4 minutes.
7. Remove the saucepan from the heat and stir in the grated cheese until melted. Season with salt and pepper.
8. Divide the cheese sauce between the two slices of toast, spreading it evenly.
9. Return the toast to the crisper basket and air fry for another 2-3 minutes, or until the cheese is bubbly and golden brown.
10. Serve immediately and enjoy!

Oatmeal breakfast bars

Serves: 6 bars

Prep time: 15 minutes / Cook time: 15 minutes

Ingredients:

- 100g rolled oats
- 50g whole wheat flour
- 1/2 tsp baking powder
- 1/2 tsp ground cinnamon
- 1/4 tsp sea salt
- 1 large egg
- 60ml maple syrup
- 30ml unsweetened almond milk
- 1 tsp vanilla extract
- 50g chopped mixed nuts and seeds
- 50g dried fruit, such as raisins or chopped dates

Instructions:

1. Preheat the air fryer to 160°C.
2. In a large bowl, whisk together the rolled oats, whole wheat flour, baking powder, cinnamon, and salt.
3. In a separate bowl, whisk together the egg, maple syrup, almond milk, and vanilla extract.
4. Add the wet Ingredients to the dry Ingredients and mix well to combine.
5. Fold in the chopped nuts, seeds, and dried fruit.
6. Line a 20x20cm baking dish with parchment paper.
7. Pour the oat mixture into the dish and smooth out the top.
8. Place the dish in the crisper basket and air fry for 12-15 minutes, or until the bars are golden brown and firm to the touch.
9. Remove the dish from the air fryer and let cool completely.
10. Cut the bars into 6 equal pieces and serve.

Breakfast egg rolls

Serves: 4

Prep time: 20 minutes / Cook time: 12 minutes

Ingredients:

- 4 large eggs
- 50ml milk
- 38g diced red pepper
- 35g diced green onion
- 25g diced cooked ham
- 1 tbsp soy sauce
- 1 tsp sesame oil
- 1 tsp grated fresh ginger
- 8 egg roll wrappers

Instructions:

1. In a bowl, whisk together eggs and milk.
2. Stir in red pepper, green onion, and cooked ham.
3. Add soy sauce, sesame oil, and grated ginger.
4. Mix until well combined.
5. Place an egg roll wrapper on a clean work surface, with one corner facing you.
6. Spoon the egg mixture onto the wrapper, in the centre. Roll the wrapper around the filling, tucking in the sides as you go, and moisten the

edges with water to seal.

7. Repeat with the remaining wrappers and filling.
8. Preheat the air fryer to 190°C.
9. Arrange the egg rolls on the crisper plate and spray them with cooking oil.
10. Air fry for 12 minutes, or until golden brown and crispy, flipping halfway through.
11. Serve with soy sauce or sweet chilli sauce, if desired.
12. Enjoy your delicious breakfast egg rolls!

Bubble and squeak patties

Serves: 4

Prep time: 10 minutes / Cook time: 20 minutes

Ingredients:

- 350g potatoes, peeled and diced
- 150g cabbage, shredded
- 1 small onion, chopped
- 50g butter, melted
- 2 tbsp plain flour
- 1 egg, beaten
- Salt and pepper, to taste
- 1 tbsp vegetable oil

Instructions:

1. Preheat the air fryer to 180°C.
2. Place the diced potatoes in a large saucepan and cover with water. Bring to a boil and cook for 10-15 minutes or until tender. Drain and mash the potatoes with a potato masher or fork.
3. In a frying pan, sauté the cabbage and onion in 1 tablespoon of vegetable oil until softened, about 5 minutes.
4. Mix the sautéed cabbage and onion with the mashed potatoes. Add the melted butter, flour, and beaten egg. Mix well and season with salt and pepper.
5. Divide the mixture into 8 equal portions and shape each into a patty.
6. Place the patties on the crisper plate and air fry for 10 minutes. Flip them over and continue cooking for another 10 minutes or until they are golden and crispy.
7. Serve hot with your preferred sauce or condiment.
8. Enjoy your Bubble and Squeak Patties!

Sweet Potato and Black Bean Enchiladas

Serves 4

Prep time: 20 minutes / Cook time: 40 minutes

Ingredients:

- 2 large sweet potatoes, peeled and diced into small cubes
- 1 can of black beans, drained and rinsed
- 1 red onion, finely chopped
- 2 cloves of garlic, minced
- 1 red bell pepper, finely chopped
- 1 jalapeño, seeded and finely chopped
- 2 tsp ground cumin
- 2 tsp smoked paprika
- 1 tsp chili powder
- 1/2 tsp ground coriander
- 1/2 tsp salt
- 1/4 tsp black pepper
- 8-10 corn tortillas
- 1 can of enchilada sauce
- 1/2 cup shredded vegan cheddar cheese

Instructions:

1. Preheat the oven to 375°F (190°C).
2. In a large skillet, heat 1 tablespoon of olive oil over medium heat. Add the onion and garlic and cook until softened, about 3-4 minutes.
3. Add the sweet potatoes, bell pepper, jalapeño, cumin, smoked paprika, chili powder, coriander, salt, and black pepper to the skillet.
4. Cook for 10-12 minutes, stirring occasionally until the sweet potatoes are tender.
5. Add the black beans to the skillet and stir to combine.
6. In a 9x13-inch baking dish, spread a thin layer of enchilada sauce on the bottom.
7. Spoon the sweet potato and black bean mixture onto each tortilla and roll up tightly. Place each enchilada seam-side down in the baking dish.
8. Pour the remaining enchilada sauce over the top of the enchiladas and sprinkle with shredded vegan cheddar cheese.
9. Cover the baking dish with foil and bake for 20-25 minutes, or until the cheese is melted and bubbly.
10. Serve hot and enjoy!

Air-fried Breakfast Sandwich with Sausage, Egg, and Cheese

Serves 1

Prep time: 10 minutes / Cook time: 12 minutes

Ingredients:

- 1 English muffin
- 1 sausage patty
- 1 large egg
- 1 slice of cheddar cheese
- Salt and pepper, to taste

Instructions:

1. Preheat your air fryer to 350°F (180°C).
2. Split the English muffin in half and toast it in the air fryer for 2-3 minutes.
3. Cook the sausage patty in the air fryer for 4-5 minutes, or until fully cooked.
4. Crack the egg into a small bowl, season with salt and pepper, and whisk with a fork.
5. Pour the egg into a small ramekin or silicone cupcake liner and place it in the air fryer.
6. Cook the egg for 3-4 minutes, or until set.
7. Assemble the breakfast sandwich by placing the cooked sausage patty and egg on one-half of the English muffin.
8. Top with a slice of cheddar cheese and the other half off the English muffin.
9. Place the assembled sandwich in the air fryer and cook for 2-3 minutes, or until the cheese is melted and the sandwich is heated through.
10. Serve hot and enjoy!

Air-fried Cinnamon Rolls

Serves 4

Prep time: 5 minutes / Cook time: 8 minutes

Ingredients:

- 1 can of refrigerated cinnamon rolls
- Cooking spray
- Powdered sugar, for garnish (optional)

Instructions:

1. Preheat your air fryer to 350°F (180°C).
2. Spray the air fryer basket with cooking spray to prevent sticking.
3. Place the cinnamon rolls in the air fryer basket, leaving some space between them.
4. Cook the cinnamon rolls for 7-8 minutes, or until golden brown and cooked through.
5. Remove the cinnamon rolls from the air fryer and let them cool for a few minutes.
6. Dust with powdered sugar, if desired.
7. Serve warm and enjoy!

Air-fried Welsh Rarebit

Serves 2

Prep time: 10 minutes / Cook time: 10 minutes

Ingredients:

- 2 thick slices of bread
- 1 tablespoon all-purpose flour
- 1/2 cup milk
- 1/2 cup grated cheddar cheese
- 1 teaspoon Dijon mustard
- Salt and pepper, to taste

Instructions:

1. Preheat your air fryer to 350°F (180°C).
2. Melt the butter in a saucepan over medium heat.
3. Whisk in the flour and cook for 1-2 minutes, or until the mixture is golden brown.
4. Gradually whisk in the milk, stirring constantly to prevent lumps.
5. Cook the mixture for 3-4 minutes, or until thickened.
6. Stir in the grated cheddar cheese and Dijon mustard until fully melted and combined.
7. Season with salt and pepper to taste.
8. Toast the bread in the air fryer for 2-3 minutes.
9. Spread the Welsh rarebit sauce on top of each slice of toast.
10. Place the toast back in the air fryer and cook for an additional 2-3 minutes

Air Fried Bubble and Squeak

Serves 2

Prep time: 10 minutes / Cook time: 15 minutes

Ingredients:

- 2 thick slices of bread
- 300g mashed potatoes
- 200g cooked cabbage or Brussels sprouts
- 1 small onion, finely chopped
- 1 tbsp vegetable oil
- Salt and pepper to taste

Instructions:

1. In a large mixing bowl, combine the 300g mashed potatoes, 200g cooked cabbage or Brussels sprouts, and finely chopped onion. Season with salt and pepper to taste.
2. Form the mixture into small patties, about 5cm in diameter and 2cm thick.
3. Brush each patty with vegetable oil on both sides. Place the patties in a single layer in the air fryer basket.
4. Cook for 5-7 minutes, then flip the patties over and cook for an additional 5-7 minutes or until crispy and golden brown.
5. Remove the patties from the air fryer and serve

Air Fried Breakfast Casserole

Serves 4

Prep time: 15 minutes / Cook time: 20 minutes

Ingredients:

- 4 slices of bread, cut into cubes
- 4 eggs
- 200ml milk
- 50g grated cheddar cheese
- 4 cooked breakfast sausages, sliced
- 1 small onion, finely chopped
- 1 tbsp vegetable oil
- Salt and pepper to taste

Instructions:

1. In a large mixing bowl, whisk together the eggs and milk. Season with salt and pepper to taste.
2. Add the cubed bread, grated cheddar cheese, sliced breakfast sausages, and finely chopped onion to the egg mixture. Stir to combine.
3. Pour the mixture into a small baking dish that will fit inside your air fryer basket.
4. Place the baking dish in the air fryer basket and cook for 20-25 minutes, or until the casserole is set and golden brown on top.
5. Remove the breakfast casserole from the air fryer and let it cool for a few minutes before slicing and serving.

Air Fried Kedgeree

Serves 4

Prep time: 10 minutes / Cook time: 20 minutes

Ingredients:

- 200g smoked haddock fillet
- 200g basmati rice
- 400ml water
- 1 small onion, finely chopped
- 1 garlic clove, minced
- 1 tsp curry powder
- 1 tbsp vegetable oil
- Salt and pepper to taste
- 2 hard-boiled eggs, chopped
- 2 tbsp chopped fresh parsley

Instructions:

1. In a large mixing bowl, soak the smoked haddock fillet in cold water for 10 minutes.
2. Rinse the basmati rice under cold water and drain.
3. In a saucepan, bring the water to a boil and add the basmati rice. Reduce the heat and simmer for 10-12 minutes, or until the rice is tender and the water has been absorbed.
4. In a small frying pan, heat the vegetable oil over medium heat. Add the chopped onion and minced garlic and cook for 2-3 minutes, or until softened.
5. Add the curry powder to the frying pan and cook for an additional 1-2 minutes, or until fragrant.
6. Drain the soaked haddock fillet and add it to the frying pan with the onion mixture. Cook for 3-4 minutes, or until the haddock is cooked through and flaky.
7. Add the cooked basmati rice to the frying pan and stir to combine with the haddock and onion mixture.
8. Season with salt and pepper to taste.
9. Transfer the kedgeree mixture to a small baking dish that will fit inside your air fryer basket.
10. Place the baking dish in the air fryer basket

Cook for 10-12 minutes, or until the kedgeree is heated through and the top is lightly golden brown and crispy.

11. Remove the kedgeree from the air fryer and sprinkle chopped fresh coriander on top.

Serve immediately with lemon wedges on the side. Enjoy!

Bacon Muffin Sandwiches

Serves 4

Prep time: 5 minutes / Cook time: 8 minutes

Ingredients:

- 4 English muffins, split
- 8 bacon medallions
- 4 slices cheese
- Cooking spray

Instructions:

1. Preheat the air fryer to 188°C.
2. Make the sandwiches: Top each of 4 muffin halves with 2 slices of Canadian bacon, 1 slice of cheese, and finish with the remaining muffin half.
3. Put the sandwiches in the air fryer basket and spritz the tops with cooking spray.
4. Bake for 4 minutes. Flip the sandwiches and bake for another 4 minutes.
5. Divide the sandwiches among four plates and serve warm.

Air Fryer Pancakes With Blueberries

Serves 4

Prep time: 10 minutes / Cook time: 14 minutes

Ingredients:

- 50g plain flour
- 10g butter, melted and slightly cooled (melted)
- 2 eggs
- 75g milk, unsweetened vanilla or flavoured
- 1g salt
- 100g blueberries

Instructions:

1. Preheat the air fryer to 270 °C . Pour the flour into a bowl and mix in the butter, eggs, milk, salt and vanilla or flavoured milk. Stir until it forms into a thin paste. Add more flour if the mixture is too runny.
2. Preheat pan on the stove and spray with oil. Lightly spoon mixture onto pan and cook until browned. Flip over and repeat with other side.
3. Add blueberries to the pancakes and enjoy.

Cheesy Cauliflower "Hash Browns"

Prep time: 30 minutes | Cook time: 24 minutes | Makes 6 hash browns

Ingredients:

- 60 g 100% cheese crisps
- 1 (340 g) steam bag cauliflower, cooked according to package Instructions
- 1 large egg
- 60 g shredded sharp Cheddar cheese
- ½ teaspoon salt

Instructions:

1. Let cooked cauliflower cool 10 minutes.
2. Place cheese crisps into food processor and pulse on low 30 seconds until crisps are finely ground.
3. Using a kitchen towel, wring out excess moisture from cauliflower and place into food processor.
4. Add egg to food processor and sprinkle with Cheddar and salt. Pulse five times until mixture is mostly smooth.
5. Cut two pieces of baking paper to fit air fryer basket. Separate mixture into six even scoops and place three on each piece of ungreased baking paper, keeping at least 2 inch of space between each scoop. Press each into a hash brown shape, about ¼ inch thick. 6. Place one batch on baking paper into air fryer basket. Adjust the temperature to 192°C and air fry for 12 minutes, turning hash browns halfway through cooking. Hash browns will be golden brown when done. Repeat with second batch.
6. Allow 5 minutes to cool. Serve warm.

Chapter 2: BBQ

Korean-style short ribs

Serves: 2

Prep time: 10 minutes / Cook time: 20 minutes

Ingredients:

- 500g beef short ribs
- 3 tablespoons soy sauce
- 2 tablespoons honey
- 2 tablespoons sesame oil
- 2 cloves garlic, minced
- 1 teaspoon grated ginger
- 1 tablespoon rice vinegar
- 1 tablespoon gochujang (Korean chilli paste)
- 1 tablespoon sesame seeds
- Salt and black pepper, to taste

Instructions:

1. In a bowl, mix together soy sauce, honey, sesame oil, garlic, ginger, rice vinegar, gochujang, sesame seeds, salt, and black pepper.
2. Add the short ribs to the marinade and toss to coat well. Let the ribs marinate for at least 1 hour in the refrigerator.
3. Preheat the air fryer to 200°C for 5 minutes.
4. Remove the ribs from the marinade and pat them dry with paper towels.
5. Place the short ribs in the air fryer basket and cook for 10 minutes, then flip them over and cook for an additional 10 minutes.
6. Once the short ribs are cooked, let them rest for 5 minutes before serving. Garnish with sesame seeds and chopped scallions.

Grilled octopus

Serves: 2

Prep time: 10 minutes / Cook time: 15 minutes

Ingredients:

- 2 small octopus tentacles
- 2 cloves garlic, minced
- 2 tablespoons olive oil
- 2 tablespoons lemon juice
- Salt and black pepper, to taste

Instructions:

1. Preheat the air fryer to 200°C for 5 minutes.
2. Clean the octopus tentacles and pat them dry with paper towels.
3. In a bowl, mix together minced garlic, olive oil, lemon juice, salt, and black pepper.
4. Brush the garlic mixture over the octopus tentacles.
5. Place the tentacles in the air fryer basket and cook for 5 minutes.
6. Flip the tentacles over and cook for an additional 5 minutes.
7. Once the octopus is cooked, let it rest for 5 minutes before serving. Garnish with lemon wedges and parsley.

Air Fryer BBQ Pulled Chicken

Serves: 4

Prep time: 10 minutes / Cook time: 20-25 minutes

Ingredients:

- 4 boneless, skinless chicken breasts (approx. 700 g)
- 25ml BBQ sauce
- 60ml ketchup
- 1 tbsp honey
- 2 tsp apple cider vinegar
- 1 tsp smoked paprika
- 1 tsp garlic powder
- Salt and pepper, to taste

Instructions:

1. In a mixing bowl, whisk together BBQ sauce, ketchup, honey, apple cider vinegar, smoked paprika, garlic powder, salt, and pepper.
2. Add chicken breasts to the bowl and coat evenly with the sauce mixture.
3. Place the chicken in the air fryer basket and cook at 190°C for 20-25 minutes, flipping the chicken halfway through cooking.

4. Once cooked, remove the chicken from the air fryer and allow it to cool for 5 minutes.
5. Using two forks, shred the chicken into bite-sized pieces.
6. Serve the pulled chicken on a bun with additional BBQ sauce, coleslaw, or your favourite toppings. Enjoy!

Spicy lamb skewers

Serves: 2

Prep time: 10 minutes

Ingredients:

- 226g ground lamb
- 1 tablespoon chilli flakes
- 1 tablespoon paprika
- 1 tablespoon cumin
- 1 tablespoon garlic powder
- Salt and pepper to taste
- 1 tablespoon olive oil
- Wooden skewers

Instructions:

1. Soak wooden skewers in water for at least 30 minutes to prevent them from burning in the air fryer.
2. In a large bowl, combine the ground lamb, chilli flakes, paprika, cumin, garlic powder, salt, and pepper. Mix well to incorporate all the Ingredients.
3. Divide the lamb mixture into 4-6 portions and shape them into long, thin sausage shapes.
4. Thread the lamb sausages onto the soaked wooden skewers.
5. Brush the lamb skewers with olive oil on all sides.
6. Preheat the air fryer to 190°C.
7. Place the lamb skewers in the air fryer basket and cook for 8-10 minutes, turning halfway through, until the lamb is cooked through and the skewers are lightly charred.
8. Serve the spicy lamb skewers hot with your favourite dipping sauce or a side of rice or salad.
9. Enjoy your delicious and easy-to-make spicy lamb skewers!

Grilled oysters

Serves: 2

Prep time: 15 minutes / Cook time: 5 minutes

Ingredients:

- 6 fresh oysters, shucked
- 1 garlic clove, minced
- 2 tablespoons fresh parsley, chopped
- 2 tablespoons unsalted butter, softened
- Salt and pepper, to taste
- Lemon wedges, for serving

Instructions:

1. In a small bowl, combine the minced garlic, chopped parsley, softened butter, salt, and pepper. Mix well to form a paste.
2. Spread the garlic butter mixture over the shucked oysters.
3. Preheat the air fryer to 200°C.
4. Place the prepared oysters in the air fryer basket and cook for 4-5 minutes, or until the butter is melted and the oysters are heated through.
5. Serve the grilled oysters hot with lemon wedges on the side.
6. Enjoy this delicious and easy-to-make grilled oyster dish as an appetiser or as part of a seafood feast!

Smoky pork shoulder

Serves: 4-6

Prep time: 15 minutes / Cook time: 2 hours

Ingredients:

1.5 kg pork shoulder, bone-in
- 1 tablespoon smoked paprika
- 1 tablespoon garlic powder
- 1 tablespoon onion powder
- 1 tablespoon brown sugar
- Salt and pepper, to taste

Instructions:

1. In a small bowl, combine the smoked paprika, garlic powder, onion powder, brown sugar, salt, and pepper. Mix well to form a rub.

2. Rub the seasoning mixture all over the pork shoulder, making sure to coat all sides.
3. Preheat the air fryer to 350°F.
4. Place the seasoned pork shoulder in the air fryer basket and cook for 2 hours, or until the internal temperature reaches 160°F.
5. Let the pork shoulder rest for 10-15 minutes before slicing and serving.
6. Enjoy this smoky and flavourful pork shoulder with your favourite sides for a delicious and satisfying meal!

Tandoori chicken

Serves: 4

Prep time: 15 minutes / Cook time: 20 minutes

Ingredients:

- 4 bone-in chicken thighs
- 400g plain Greek yoghurt
- 2 tablespoons lemon juice
- 1 tablespoon grated ginger
- 1 tablespoon garam masala
- 1 tablespoon ground cumin
- 1 tablespoon smoked paprika
- 1 tablespoon garlic powder
- Salt and pepper, to taste
- 2 teaspoons olive oil

Instructions:

1. In a large bowl, whisk together the Greek yoghurt, lemon juice, grated ginger, garam masala, cumin, smoked paprika, garlic powder, salt, and pepper to form a marinade.
2. Add the chicken thighs to the marinade, making sure to coat them well. Cover and refrigerate for at least 1 hour, or overnight for best results.
3. Preheat the air fryer to 180°C.
4. Remove the chicken thighs from the marinade and shake off any excess.
5. Brush the chicken thighs with olive oil on all sides.
6. Place the chicken thighs in the air fryer basket and cook for 20 minutes, turning halfway through, or until the internal temperature reaches 75°C.
7. Let the chicken thighs rest for 5-10 minutes before serving.

8. Enjoy this delicious and flavourful tandoori chicken with your favourite sides for a delicious and satisfying meal!

Moroccan-style grilled vegetables

Serves: 2

Prep time: 15 minutes / Cook time: 10 minutes

Ingredients:

- 1 red pepper, seeded and sliced
- 1 yellow pepper, seeded and sliced
- 1 courgette, sliced diagonally
- 1 small red onion, cut into wedges
- 2 tbsp olive oil
- 1 tsp ground cumin
- 1 tsp ground coriander
- 1 tsp smoked paprika
- 1/2 tsp ground cinnamon
- Sea salt and black pepper, to taste
- 2 tbsp chopped fresh parsley
- 2 tbsp chopped fresh mint
- Lemon wedges, to serve

Instructions:

1. Preheat the air fryer to 200°C.
2. In a large bowl, mix together the olive oil, cumin, coriander, smoked paprika, cinnamon, salt, and pepper.
3. Add the sliced vegetables and toss to coat well.
4. Arrange the vegetables on the crisper plate and place it in the air fryer basket.
5. Select "AIR FRY" and cook for 10 minutes, shaking the basket occasionally.
6. Remove the vegetables from the air fryer and sprinkle them with chopped parsley and mint.
7. Serve hot with lemon wedges.

Grilled prawns with garlic and lemon

Serves: 2

Prep time: 10 minutes / Cook time: 5 minutes

Ingredients:

- 12 large raw prawns, peeled and deveined

- 2 garlic cloves, minced
- 1 tbsp olive oil
- 1 tbsp lemon juice
- 1/2 tsp smoked paprika
- Sea salt and black pepper, to taste
- 2 tbsp chopped fresh parsley
- Lemon wedges, to serve

Instructions:

1. Preheat the air fryer to 200°C.
2. In a bowl, mix together the garlic, olive oil, lemon juice, smoked paprika, salt, and pepper.
3. Add the prawns and toss to coat well.
4. Arrange the prawns on the crisper plate and place it in the air fryer basket.
5. Select air fry and cook for 5 minutes, shaking the basket occasionally.
6. Remove the prawns from the air fryer and sprinkle them with chopped parsley.
7. Serve hot with lemon wedges.

Charred halloumi skewers

Serves: 2

Prep time: 15 minutes / Cook time: 8 minutes

Ingredients:

- 150g halloumi cheese, cut into 12 cubes
- 1 red onion, cut into wedges
- 1 red pepper, seeded and cut into 12 pieces
- 2 tbsp olive oil
- 1 tsp dried oregano
- 1/2 tsp smoked paprika
- Sea salt and black pepper, to taste
- Lemon wedges, to serve

Instructions:

1. Preheat the air fryer to 200°C.
2. In a bowl, mix together the olive oil, oregano, smoked paprika, salt, and pepper.
3. Add the halloumi cubes, onion wedges, and red pepper pieces, and toss to coat well.
4. Thread the halloumi, onion, and red pepper onto skewers, alternating between the Ingredients.
5. Arrange the skewers on the crisper plate and place it in the air fryer basket.
6. Select air fry and cook for 8 minutes, shaking the

basket occasionally.
7. Remove the skewers from the air fryer and serve hot with lemon wedges.

Jerk chicken wings

Serves: 4

Prep time: 15 minutes / Cook time: 20 minutes

Ingredients:

- 12 chicken wings
- 2 tbsp jerk seasoning
- 1 tbsp vegetable oil

Instructions:

1. Combine the chicken wings, jerk seasoning, and vegetable oil in a mixing bowl, and toss to coat.
2. Arrange the chicken wings on the crisper plate and select "AIR FRY" at 200°C for 20 minutes.
3. Select "START/STOP" to begin cooking.
4. When the timer beeps, check the chicken wings with a meat thermometer to ensure they have reached an internal temperature of 75°C.
5. Serve hot with your favourite dipping sauce.

Grilled salmon with herb butter

Serves: 2

Prep time: 10 minutes / Cook time: 12 minutes

Ingredients:

- 2 salmon fillets (150g each)
- 2 tbsp butter, softened
- 1 tbsp chopped fresh herbs (such as parsley, chives, and dill)
- 1 garlic clove, minced
- Sea salt and ground black pepper, to taste

Instructions:

1. Pat salmon fillets dry using paper towels, and season with salt and pepper.
2. In a small mixing bowl, combine the softened butter, chopped herbs, minced garlic, salt, and pepper to make the herb butter.

3. Arrange the salmon fillets on the crisper plate and spread the herb butter on top of each fillet.
4. Select air fry at 200°C for 12 minutes.
5. When the timer beeps, check the salmon fillets with a fork to ensure they are flaky and cooked through.
6. Serve hot with your favourite side dish.

BBQ beef brisket

Serves: 6

Prep time: 10 minutes / Cook time: 1 hour and 45 minutes

Ingredients:

1.5kg beef brisket
- 2 tbsp BBQ rub
- 120ml BBQ sauce
- Tomato Ketchup (Optional for serving)
- Salt and Black Pepper (Optional for serving)

Instructions:

1. Pat the beef brisket dry using paper towels, and rub the BBQ rub all over the brisket.
2. Place the beef brisket on the crisper plate and select air fry at 160°C for 1 hour.
3. After the initial hour of cooking at 160°C, increase the temperature to 180°C and continue cooking the beef brisket for another 45 minutes, or until the internal temperature of the brisket reaches 93°C.
4. Once the brisket is cooked, remove it from the crisper plate and let it rest for 10-15 minutes before slicing it against the grain.
5. Serve the sliced brisket with the BBQ sauce drizzled over the top, and any additional sides of your choice such as coleslaw, baked beans, or corn on the cob. Enjoy!

Grilled peaches with vanilla ice cream

Serves: 4

Prep time: 5 minutes / Cook time: 6 minutes

Ingredients:

- 4 ripe peaches, halved and pitted
- 2 tbsp honey
- 1 tsp ground cinnamon
- Vanilla ice cream, to serve

Instructions:

1. Preheat the Air Fryer to 180°C.
2. In a small bowl, mix together honey and cinnamon until well combined.
3. Brush the cut side of each peach half with the honey-cinnamon mixture.
4. Arrange the peaches, cut-side up, on the crisper plate.
5. Select air fry at 180°C for 6 minutes.
6. Serve the grilled peaches warm with a scoop of vanilla ice cream.

Chapter 3: Family Favourites

Turkey and stuffing meatballs

Serves: 4

Prep time: 10 minutes / Cook time: 15 minutes

Ingredients:

- 500g turkey mince
- 120g stuffing mix
- 1 egg, lightly beaten
- 2 tbsp chopped fresh parsley
- 1 tsp salt
- 1/2 tsp black pepper

Instructions:

1. Preheat the Air Fryer to 180°C.
2. In a large bowl, mix together turkey mince, stuffing mix, beaten egg, parsley, salt, and pepper until well combined.
3. Shape the mixture into 16 meatballs.
4. Place the meatballs on the crisper plate.
5. Select air fry at 180°C for 15 minutes or until cooked through.
6. Serve the meatballs hot with your favourite dipping sauce.

Cheese and onion pasties

Serves: 4

Prep time: 20 minutes / Cook time: 25 minutes

Ingredients:

- 250g plain flour
- 125g unsalted butter, cold and cubed
- 1 tsp salt
- 50ml cold water
- 1 large onion, chopped
- 100g grated Cheddar cheese
- 1 egg, lightly beaten
- 1 tbsp milk

Instructions:

1. Preheat the Air Fryer to 180°C.
2. In a large bowl, mix together flour, butter, and salt until the mixture resembles breadcrumbs.
3. Add water gradually, mixing until the dough comes together.
4. Roll out the dough on a lightly floured surface to about 3mm thickness.
5. Cut out 4 circles (about 15 cm in diameter) from the dough.
6. In a small bowl, mix together chopped onion and grated cheese.
7. Divide the cheese and onion mixture among the 4 dough circles.
8. Fold the dough over the filling to create a half-moon shape and crimp the edges to seal.
9. Whisk together the egg and milk in a small bowl.
10. Brush the pasties with the egg wash.
11. Place the pasties on the crisper plate.
12. Select air fry at 180°C for 25 minutes or until golden brown.
13. Serve the cheese and onion pasties hot or cold.

Air fryer garlic shrimp

Serves: 2

Prep time: 5 minutes / Cook time: 10 minutes

Ingredients:

- 200g raw shrimp, peeled and deveined
- 1 tbsp olive oil
- 2 garlic cloves, minced
- 1 tsp paprika
- 1/4 tsp salt
- 1/4 tsp black pepper
- Lemon wedges, for serving

Instructions:

1. In a mixing bowl, combine the shrimp, olive oil, garlic, paprika, salt, and black pepper.
2. Toss well to coat the shrimp evenly.
3. Arrange the shrimp in a single layer on the crisper plate of the air fryer.
4. Select air fry at 200°C for 10 minutes.
5. After 5 minutes, use silicone-tipped tongs to flip the shrimp over.
6. Continue cooking for the remaining 5 minutes.
7. Serve hot with lemon wedges for a squeeze of fresh juice over the top. Enjoy!

Air fryer shepherd's pie

Serves: 4

Prep time: 15 minutes / Cook time: 25 minutes

Ingredients:

- 500g ground lamb
- 1 onion, finely chopped
- 1 carrot, peeled and finely chopped
- 1 celery stalk, finely chopped
- 2 garlic cloves, minced
- 2 tbsp tomato paste
- 1 tsp dried thyme
- 1 tsp dried rosemary
- 1 tsp salt
- 1/2 tsp black pepper
- 400g potatoes, peeled and cubed
- 1 tbsp butter
- 1/4 cup milk
- 50g grated cheddar cheese

Instructions:

1. In a large non-stick skillet, cook the ground lamb over medium heat until browned, stirring occasionally, for about 5-7 minutes.
2. Add the chopped onion, carrot, and celery, and cook until the vegetables soften, stirring occasionally, for about 5 minutes.
3. Add the minced garlic, tomato paste, thyme, rosemary, salt, and black pepper, and cook for 2 more minutes, stirring occasionally.
4. In a mixing bowl, combine the cubed potatoes, butter, milk, and grated cheddar cheese, and mash them until smooth.
5. Grease the crisper plate of the air fryer with a little bit of oil.
6. Add the meat and vegetable mixture to the bottom of the plate, and spread it evenly.
7. Spread the mashed potato mixture on top of the meat and vegetables, and smooth it out.
8. Select air fry at 180°C for 25 minutes.
9. After 15 minutes, use a fork to score the surface of the mashed potato mixture.
10. Continue cooking for the remaining 10 minutes, or until the top is golden brown and the filling is bubbly. Serve hot and enjoy!

Cauliflower mac and cheese bites

Serves: 12 bites

Prep time: 10 minutes / Cook time: 18 minutes

Ingredients:

- 1 small head cauliflower, cut into small florets
- 140g macaroni
- 113 g grated cheddar cheese
- 23g grated parmesan cheese
- 25g panko breadcrumbs
- 60ml milk
- 1/2 tsp salt
- 1 egg
- 1/4 tsp black pepper

Instructions:

1. Cook the macaroni according to the package Instructions.
2. Drain and rinse with cold water.
3. Place the cauliflower florets in a microwave-safe bowl with a tablespoon of water.
4. Cover with a lid or plastic wrap and microwave on high for 3-4 minutes, until tender.
5. Drain any excess water.
6. In a mixing bowl, combine the cooked macaroni, cooked cauliflower, cheddar cheese, parmesan cheese, panko breadcrumbs, milk, egg, salt, and black pepper, and mix well.
7. Preheat your air fryer to 190°C.
8. Grease the crisper plate of the air fryer with cooking spray or oil.
9. Scoop the mac and cheese mixture into a muffin tin, filling each cup about 3/4 full.
10. Alternatively, you can use a cookie scoop to portion out the mixture onto the greased crisper plate.
11. Place the muffin tin or crisper plate in the air fryer basket and cook for 15-18 minutes, until the tops are golden brown and the bites are cooked through.
12. Serve hot and enjoy your delicious cauliflower mac and cheese bites!

Stuffed peppers

Serves: 4

Prep time: 15 minutes / Cook time: 20 minutes

Ingredients:

- 4 medium-sized bell peppers, halved lengthwise and seeded
- 1 tbsp olive oil
- 1 small onion, chopped
- 1 garlic clove, minced
- 1 cup cooked rice
- 1 cup canned black beans, rinsed and drained
- 1 cup canned diced tomatoes
- 1 tbsp chopped fresh parsley
- 1/2 tsp ground cumin
- 1/2 tsp smoked paprika
- 1/2 tsp sea salt
- 1/4 tsp black pepper
- 75g shredded cheddar cheese

Instructions:

1. Preheat your air fryer to 190°C.
2. In a large skillet, heat the olive oil over medium heat.
3. Add the onion and garlic, and cook until softened, about 3 minutes.
4. Add the cooked rice, black beans, diced tomatoes, parsley, cumin, smoked paprika, sea salt, and black pepper, and stir until well combined.
5. Stuff the mixture into the bell pepper halves, and sprinkle the shredded cheddar cheese on top.
6. Place the stuffed peppers on the crisper plate of the air fryer and cook for 20 minutes until the peppers are tender and the cheese is melted and bubbly.
7. Serve hot and enjoy your delicious stuffed peppers!

Air fryer falafel

Serves: 4

Prep time: 20 minutes / Cook time: 12 minutes

Ingredients:

- 1 can (400g) chickpeas, drained and rinsed
- 1 small onion, roughly chopped
- 2 garlic cloves, minced
- 2 tbsp chopped fresh parsley
- 2 tbsp chopped fresh cilantro
- 1 tsp ground cumin
- 1/2 tsp ground coriander
- 1/4 tsp cayenne pepper
- 1/2 tsp sea salt
- 1/4 tsp black pepper
- 2 tbsp all-purpose flour
- 2 tbsp olive oil

Instructions:

1. Preheat your air fryer to 190°C.
2. In a food processor, combine the chickpeas, onion, garlic, parsley, cilantro, cumin, coriander, cayenne pepper, sea salt, black pepper, and all-purpose flour, and pulse until the mixture is well combined but still slightly chunky.
3. Using your hands, shape the mixture into small balls or patties.
4. Place the falafel balls or patties on the crisper plate of the air fryer and brush them with olive oil.
5. Cook for 12 minutes, turning them halfway through the cooking time, until they are crispy and golden brown.
6. Serve hot with your favourite dipping sauce and enjoy your delicious air fryer falafel!

Air fryer chicken and waffles

Serves: 4

Prep time: 15 minutes / Cook time: 18 minutes

Ingredients:

For the chicken:

- 4 boneless, skinless chicken breasts
- 240m buttermilk
- 1 tbsp paprika
- 1 tbsp onion powder
- 1/2 tsp black pepper
- For the waffles:
- 2 tbsp sugar
- 1/2 tsp sea salt
- 2 eggs
- 60g unsalted butter, melted
- 1 tsp vanilla extract
- 125g all-purpose flour
- 1 tbsp garlic powder
- 1 tsp sea salt
- Cooking spray
- 250g all-purpose flour
- 1 tbsp baking powder
- 420ml milk

Instructions:

1. Preheat your air fryer to 190°C.
2. In a shallow dish, marinate the chicken breasts in buttermilk for at least 30 minutes.
3. In another shallow dish, mix the flour, paprika, garlic powder, onion powder, sea salt, and black

pepper.

4. Remove the chicken breasts from the buttermilk and dredge them in the flour mixture, shaking off any excess flour.

5. Spray the air fryer basket with cooking spray and place the chicken breasts inside.

6. Spray the top of the chicken with additional cooking spray.

7. Cook for 15-20 minutes, or until the internal temperature of the chicken reaches 74°C and the coating is crispy and golden brown.

8. While the chicken is cooking, make the waffle batter.

9. In a large bowl, whisk together the flour, sugar, baking powder, and sea salt.

10. In a separate bowl, whisk together the milk, eggs, melted butter, and vanilla extract.

11. Pour the wet Ingredients into the dry Ingredients and stir until just combined.

12. Pour the waffle batter into a preheated waffle iron and cook according to the manufacturer's Instructions.

13. Serve the air fryer chicken with the waffles and your favourite toppings, such as syrup, honey, or hot sauce. Enjoy!

Buffalo chicken strips

Serves: 2

Prep time: 15 minutes / Cook time: 12 minutes

Ingredients:

- 2 chicken breasts (300g), cut into strips
- 50g plain flour
- 1 tsp paprika
- 1/2 tsp garlic powder
- 1/2 tsp onion powder
- 1/2 tsp dried thyme
- 1/2 tsp salt
- 1/4 tsp black pepper
- 1 large egg, beaten
- 50g breadcrumbs
- 50g buffalo sauce
- 1 tbsp unsalted butter, melted

Instructions:

1. Preheat the air fryer to 200°C.

2. In a shallow dish, mix the flour, paprika, garlic powder, onion powder, dried thyme, salt, and black pepper.

3. In another shallow dish, beat the egg. In a third shallow dish, add the breadcrumbs.

4. Dust each chicken strip with the flour mixture, then dip them in the egg, and roll them over the breadcrumbs, pressing gently to adhere.

5. Place the chicken strips in the air fryer basket, leaving some space in between.

6. Air fry for 10 minutes.

7. In a small bowl, mix the buffalo sauce and melted butter.

8. Brush the chicken strips with the buffalo sauce mixture and air fry for another 2 minutes.

9. Serve hot with your favourite dipping sauce.

Air fryer pizza

Serves: 2

Prep time: 10 minutes / Cook time: 8 minutes

Ingredients:

- 150g pizza dough
- 4 tbsp tomato sauce
- 50g mozzarella cheese, shredded
- 1/4 tsp dried oregano
- 1/4 tsp garlic powder
- 1/4 tsp onion powder
- 1/4 tsp salt
- 1/8 tsp black pepper
- 1 tsp olive oil

Instructions:

1. Preheat the air fryer to 200°C.

2. Roll out the pizza dough on a floured surface to the desired thickness.

3. Spread the tomato sauce on the pizza dough, leaving a small border around the edges.

4. Sprinkle the shredded mozzarella cheese on top of the sauce.

5. In a small bowl, mix the dried oregano, garlic powder, onion powder, salt, and black pepper.

6. Sprinkle the spice mixture on top of the cheese.

7. Drizzle the olive oil on top of the pizza.

8. Place the pizza in the air fryer basket and air fry for 8 minutes.

9. Slice and serve hot.

Air fryer sweet potato fries

Serves: 2

Prep time: 10 minutes / Cook time: 18 minutes

Ingredients:

- 450g sweet potatoes, peeled and cut into thin fries

- 1 tbsp cornstarch
- 1/2 tsp garlic powder
- 1/2 tsp salt
- 1 tbsp olive oil
- 1 tsp paprika
- 1/2 tsp onion powder
- 1/4 tsp black pepper

Instructions:

1. Preheat the air fryer to 200°C.
2. In a large bowl, mix the sweet potato fries, cornstarch, paprika, garlic powder, onion powder, salt, and black pepper until the fries are evenly coated.
3. Drizzle the olive oil on top of the sweet potato fries and toss to combine.
4. Place the sweet potato fries in the air fryer basket and air fry for 16-18 minutes, shaking the basket every 5 minutes to ensure even cooking.
5. Serve hot with your favourite dipping sauce.

Air fryer quiche

Serves: 4-6

Prep time: 15 minutes / Cook time: 20 minutes

Ingredients:

- 4 eggs
- 80g grated cheddar cheese
- 50g diced ham
- 1/4 tsp black pepper
- 1 ready-made pie crust
- 1 tsp olive oil
- 120ml milk
- 1/4 tsp salt
- 1/4 tsp garlic powder

Instructions:

1. Preheat your air fryer to 180°C for 5 minutes.
2. In a mixing bowl, whisk together the eggs, milk, salt, black pepper, and garlic powder.
3. Add the grated cheese and diced ham, and stir well to combine.
4. Grease a 7-inch pie dish with olive oil and place the ready-made pie crust inside.
5. Pour the egg and cheese mixture into the pie crust.
6. Place the pie dish inside the air fryer basket and cook for 20 minutes or until the quiche is set and the crust is golden brown.
7. Allow the quiche to cool for a few minutes before slicing and serving.

Air fryer cornbread

Serves: 4-6

Prep time: 10 minutes / Cook time: 15 minutes

Ingredients:

- 120g cornmeal
- 1 tbsp sugar
- 1/4 tsp baking soda
- 120ml buttermilk
- 2 tbsp melted butter
- 80g plain flour
- 1 tsp baking powder
- 1/4 tsp salt
- 2 eggs
- 1 tsp olive oil

Instructions:

1. Preheat your air fryer to 180°C for 5 minutes.
2. In a mixing bowl, combine the cornmeal, flour, sugar, baking powder, baking soda, and salt.
3. In a separate bowl, whisk together the buttermilk, eggs, and melted butter.
4. Add the wet Ingredients to the dry Ingredients and stir well to combine.
5. Grease a 6-inch round cake pan with olive oil and pour the cornbread batter inside.
6. Place the cake pan inside the air fryer basket and cook for 15 minutes or until a toothpick inserted in the centre comes out clean.
7. Remove the cornbread from the air fryer and allow it to cool for a few minutes before slicing and serving.

Chicken curry

Serves 4

Prep time: 20 minutes / Cook Time: 30 minutes

Ingredients:

- 500g boneless, skinless chicken breasts or thighs, cut into bite-sized pieces
- 2 tablespoons vegetable oil
- 1 large onion, chopped
- 3 garlic cloves, minced
- 1 tablespoon grated fresh ginger
- 2 teaspoons ground cumin
- 2 teaspoons ground coriander
- 1 teaspoon ground turmeric
- 1/2 teaspoon red pepper flakes (optional)
- 480ml chicken broth
- 400g diced tomatoes, undrained

- 400g chickpeas, drained and rinsed
- 240ml coconut milk
- Salt and black pepper, to taste
- Fresh cilantro leaves, chopped, for garnish

Instructions:

1. Heat the oil in a large pot or Dutch oven over medium heat. Add the onion and cook until softened, about 5 minutes. Add the garlic and ginger and cook for an additional 1-2 minutes until fragrant.
2. Add the chicken to the pot and cook until browned on all sides, about 5-7 minutes.
3. Add the cumin, coriander, turmeric, and red pepper flakes (if using) to the pot and stir to combine.
4. Pour in the chicken broth, diced tomatoes, and chickpeas. Bring to a boil, then reduce heat and let simmer for 15-20 minutes.
5. Stir in the coconut milk and let cook for an additional 5-10 minutes, or until the chicken is cooked through and the sauce has thickened slightly.
6. Season with salt and black pepper to taste.
7. Serve hot over rice, garnished with fresh cilantro leaves. Enjoy your delicious homemade chicken curry!

Air Fryer Fruit and Pork Kebabs

Serves: 4

Prep time: 20 minutes / Cook time: 12 minutes

Ingredients:

- 400g pork tenderloin, cut into bite-size cubes
- 1 red pepper, cut into bite-size pieces
- 1 green pepper, cut into bite-size pieces
- 1 small red onion, cut into bite-size pieces
- 8 cherry tomatoes
- 8 pineapple chunks
- 2 tbsp olive oil
- 1 tbsp honey
- 1 tbsp soy sauce
- 1 tsp garlic powder
- 1/4 tsp salt
- 1/4 tsp black pepper
- 4 wooden skewers

Instructions:

1. Soak the wooden skewers in water for at least 30 minutes before using.

2. In a mixing bowl, whisk together the olive oil, honey, soy sauce, garlic powder, salt, and black pepper.
3. Add the pork, peppers, red onion, cherry tomatoes, and pineapple chunks to the bowl and toss well to coat.
4. Thread the marinated pork and vegetables onto the soaked wooden skewers, alternating between the different Ingredients.
5. Preheat your air fryer to 200°C for 5 minutes.
6. Place the skewers inside the air fryer basket and cook for 12 minutes, flipping them halfway through.
7. Remove the kebabs from the air fryer and allow them to cool for a few minutes before serving.

Shepherd's pie

Serves 4-6

Prep time: 20 minutes / Cook time: 1 hour

Ingredients:

- 800g potatoes, peeled and cubed
- 50g unsalted butter
- 1/4 cup milk
- Salt and freshly ground black pepper
- 1 tablespoon vegetable oil
- 1 onion, diced
- 2 carrots, diced
- 2 celery stalks, diced
- 2 garlic cloves, minced
- 500g ground lamb (or beef)
- 2 tablespoons all-purpose flour
- 1 tablespoon tomato paste
- 1 cup beef or chicken stock
- 1 teaspoon Worcestershire sauce
- 2 tablespoons fresh parsley leaves, chopped
- 1 tablespoon fresh thyme leaves, chopped
- 1/2 cup frozen peas

Instructions:

1. Preheat your air frye to 200°C. Place the potatoes in a large saucepan and cover with cold water. Bring to a boil and cook until tender, about 15 minutes. Drain the potatoes and mash them with butter and milk until smooth. Season with salt and pepper and set aside.

2. In a large skillet, heat the vegetable oil over medium heat. Add the onion, carrots, celery, and garlic and cook until the vegetables are tender about 5-7 minutes.

3. Add the ground lamb to the skillet and cook until browned, about 8-10 minutes, breaking up any large chunks with a spoon.

4. Sprinkle the flour over the lamb and stir until evenly distributed. Add the tomato paste, stock, Worcestershire sauce, parsley, thyme, and frozen peas. Bring to a boil, reduce heat to low, and simmer for 10-15 minutes until the sauce has thickened.

5. Transfer the lamb mixture to a large baking dish and spread the mashed potatoes over the top, smoothing it out with a fork.

6. Place the baking dish in the oven and bake for 30-35 minutes, until the top is golden brown and the filling is bubbling.

7. Remove from the oven and let it cool for a few minutes before serving.

8. Enjoy your delicious Shepherd's Pie!

Air Fryer Peach and Blueberry Crumble

Serves: 4

Prep time: 10 minutes / Cook time: 20 minutes

Ingredients:

- For the filling:
- 2 ripe peaches, peeled and chopped
- 100g blueberries
- 1 tablespoon cornstarch
- 1 tablespoon honey
- 1/2 teaspoon ground cinnamon
- Pinch of salt
- For the topping:
- 50g rolled oats
- 30g plain flour
- 2 tablespoons brown sugar
- 1/4 teaspoon ground cinnamon
- 30g unsalted butter, melted

Instructions:

1. Preheat your air fryer to 180°C.

2. In a bowl, mix the peaches, blueberries, cornstarch, honey, cinnamon, and salt.

3. In another bowl, mix the oats, flour, brown sugar, cinnamon, and melted butter until it forms a crumbly mixture.

4. Divide the fruit mixture evenly between 4 ramekins or oven-safe dishes. Sprinkle the oat mixture over the top.

5. Place the dishes in the air fryer basket and cook for 10 minutes.

6. After 10 minutes, check the crumbles. If they are not golden brown, cook for another 5-10 minutes until they are.

7. Serve the crumbles warm, topped with whipped cream or ice cream.

Radish Chips

Serves 4

Prep time: 10 minutes / Cook time: 5 minutes

Ingredients:

- 500 ml water
- 455 g radishes
- ¼ teaspoon onion powder
- ¼ teaspoon paprika
- ½ teaspoon garlic powder
- 2 tablespoons coconut oil, melted

Instructions:

1. Place water in a medium saucepan and bring to a boil on stovetop.

2. Remove the top and bottom from each radish, then use a mandoline to slice each radish thin and uniformly. You may also use the slicing blade in the food processor for this step.

3. Place the radish slices into the boiling water for 5 minutes or until translucent. Remove them from the water and place them into a clean kitchen towel to absorb excess moisture.

4. Toss the radish chips in a large bowl with remaining Ingredients until fully coated in oil and seasoning. Place radish chips into the air fryer basket.

5. Adjust the temperature to 160ºC and air fry for 5 minutes. 6. Shake the basket two or three times during the cooking time. Serve warm.

Air Fryer Apple Cinnamon French Toast

Serves: 4

Prep time: 10 minutes / Cook time: 20 minutes

Ingredients:

- 8 slices of bread, preferably brioche or challah
- 3 large eggs
- 100ml milk
- 1 teaspoon ground cinnamon
- 1 teaspoon vanilla extract
- 1 apple, peeled and sliced
- 2 tablespoons unsalted butter
- Maple syrup, to serve

Instructions:

1. In a bowl, whisk the eggs, milk, cinnamon, and vanilla extract until well combined.
2. Dip the bread slices in the egg mixture, making sure they are coated evenly on both sides.
3. Preheat your air fryer to 180°C.
4. Melt the butter in a pan over medium heat. Add the sliced apple and cook for 2-3 minutes until slightly softened.
5. Arrange the bread slices in a single layer in the air fryer basket. Cook for 5-6 minutes until the bread is crispy and golden brown.
6. Flip the bread slices over and top each slice with a few apple slices. Cook for another 3-4 minutes until the other side is crispy and golden brown.
7. Serve the French toast warm with maple syrup.

Bangers and mash

Serves 4

Prep time: 10 minutes / Cook time: 40 minutes

Ingredients:

- 8 sausages (preferably British pork sausages)
- 1 kg potatoes, peeled and cut into chunks
- 100 g unsalted butter
- 1/2 cup whole milk
- Salt and freshly ground black pepper, to taste
- 2 tbsp olive oil
- 2 large onions, peeled and sliced
- 2 garlic cloves, minced
- 2 tbsp all-purpose flour
- 1 cup beef stock
- 1 tbsp Worcestershire sauce
- 1 tbsp tomato paste
- 1 tbsp Dijon mustard
- 2 tbsp fresh parsley, chopped

Instructions:

1. Preheat your air frye to 200°C.
2. Put the potatoes in a large saucepan and cover with cold water. Add salt to taste and bring to a boil. Reduce heat and simmer for 20-25 minutes or until potatoes are tender.
3. While the potatoes are cooking, heat the olive oil in a large frying pan over medium-high heat. Add the sausages and cook for 8-10 minutes or until golden brown on all sides. Transfer the sausages to a baking dish and bake in the oven for 15 minutes.
4. In the same pan, add the onions and garlic and sauté until softened, about 5 minutes.
5. Add the flour and stir for a minute until fully combined with the onions and garlic.
6. Gradually add the beef stock, Worcestershire sauce, tomato paste, and Dijon mustard while stirring constantly until a smooth sauce is formed.
7. Add the sauce to the baking dish with the sausages.
8. Drain the potatoes and add the butter and milk. Mash the potatoes until smooth and season with salt and pepper to taste.
9. Spoon the mashed potatoes on top of the sausages and sauce, spreading evenly.
10. Bake in the oven for 20-25 minutes or until the mashed potatoes are golden brown.
11. Garnish with chopped parsley and serve hot. Enjoy your bangers and mash!

Steak and Kidney Pie

Serves 4

Prep time: 30 minutes / Cook time: 2 hours

Ingredients

- 400g beef steak, trimmed and cubed
- 200g beef kidney, trimmed and cubed

- 1 onion, chopped
- 2 cloves of garlic, minced
- 2 tbsp plain flour
- 1 tbsp tomato paste
- 1 tbsp Worcestershire sauce
- 400ml beef stock
- 2 bay leaves
- 1 sheet of ready-rolled shortcrust pastry
- 1 sheet of ready-rolled puff pastry
- 1 egg, beaten

Instructions

1. Preheat your air fryer to 180°C .
2. In a large pan, heat some oil over high heat. Add the beef steak and kidney, and cook for 5-10 minutes until browned on all sides. Remove the meat from the pan and set aside.
3. In the same pan, add the onions and garlic. Sauté for 5 minutes until soft and golden. Sprinkle the flour over the onion mixture, and stir well to combine. Add the tomato paste, Worcestershire sauce, and beef stock, stirring constantly to prevent lumps from forming. Add the bay leaves and season with salt and black pepper to taste. Bring to a simmer and cook for 5 minutes until the sauce has thickened.
4. Return the beef to the pan, and stir well to coat it in the sauce. Simmer for 30 minutes, stirring occasionally, until the meat is tender.
5. Transfer the meat mixture to a 23cm pie dish.
6. On a floured surface, roll out the shortcrust pastry to the thickness of a pound coin. Cut out a circle that is slightly larger than the rim of the pie dish. Place the circle over the meat mixture and press the edges to seal. Prick the top with a fork.
7. Roll out the puff pastry on a floured surface to the thickness of a pound coin. Cut out a circle that is slightly larger than the rim of the pie dish. Place the circle over the shortcrust pastry and press the edges to seal. Make a small hole in the center of the pie to allow steam to escape.
8. Brush the pie with beaten egg and bake in the preheated oven for 45-50 minutes or until golden brown and puffed up.
9. Remove from the oven and let it cool for a few minutes before serving. Enjoy hot!

Vegetarian shepherd's pie with lentils

Serves 4-6

Prep time: 20 minutes / Cook time: 2 hours

Ingredients:

- For the filling:
- 1 cup of green or brown lentils
- 2 tablespoons olive oil
- 1 onion, diced
- 2 cloves of garlic, minced
- 2 medium carrots, peeled and diced
- 2 stalks of celery, diced
- 1 teaspoon dried thyme
- 1 teaspoon dried rosemary
- 1 teaspoon paprika
- 2 tablespoons tomato paste
- 1 tablespoon soy sauce
- 2 cups vegetable broth
- 1 tablespoon cornstarch
- Salt and pepper to taste
- For the mashed potato topping:
- 3 medium potatoes, peeled and chopped
- 1/4 cup unsweetened plant milk
- 2 tablespoons vegan butter or olive oil
- Salt and pepper to taste

Instructions:

1. Rinse the lentils and place them in a pot with enough water to cover them by 2-3 inches. Bring to a boil, then reduce the heat and simmer for 20-25 minutes or until tender. Drain and set aside.
2. Preheat the oven to 375°F (190°C).
3. Heat the olive oil in a large skillet over medium heat. Add the onion and garlic and cook for 2-3 minutes until softened.
4. Add the carrots and celery and continue to cook for another 5-7 minutes until they begin to soften.
5. Stir in the thyme, rosemary, paprika, tomato paste, and soy sauce. Cook for 1-2 minutes until fragrant.
6. Pour in the vegetable broth and stir to combine. In a small bowl, whisk together the cornstarch

with 1 tablespoon of water until smooth. Add to the skillet and stir until the sauce thickens.

7. Add the cooked lentils to the skillet and mix until everything is combined. Season with salt and pepper to taste.

8. Meanwhile, cook the chopped potatoes in a pot of boiling water until tender. Drain and mash with the plant milk and vegan butter or olive oil until smooth. Season with salt and pepper to taste.

9. Transfer the lentil filling to a large baking dish. Spread the mashed potatoes on top, making sure to cover the filling completely.

10. Bake for 20-25 minutes or until the top is golden brown and the filling is bubbling. Let cool for a few minutes before serving. Enjoy!

Spaghetti Zoodles and Meatballs

Serves 6

Prep time: 30 minutes | Cook time: 11 to 13 minutes

Ingredients:

- 450 g minced beef
- 1½ teaspoons sea salt, plus more for seasoning
- 1 large egg, beaten
- 1 teaspoon gelatin
- 95 g Parmesan cheese
- 2 teaspoons minced garlic
- 1 teaspoon Italian seasoning
- Freshly ground black pepper, to taste
- Avocado oil spray
- Keto-friendly marinara sauce, for serving
- 170 g courgette noodles, made using a spiraliser or store-bought

Instructions:

1. Place the minced beef in a large bowl, and season with the salt.

2. Place the egg in a separate bowl and sprinkle with the gelatin. Allow to sit for 5 minutes.

3. Stir the gelatin mixture, then pour it over the minced beef. Add the Parmesan, garlic, and Italian seasoning. Season with salt and pepper.

4. Form the mixture into 1½-inch meatballs and place them on a plate; cover with plastic wrap

and refrigerate for at least 1 hour or overnight.

5. Spray the meatballs with oil. Set the air fryer to 204ºC and arrange the meatballs in a single layer in the air fryer basket. Air fry for 4 minutes. Flip the meatballs and spray them with more oil. Air fry for 4 minutes more, until an instant-read thermometer reads 72ºC. Transfer the meatballs to a plate and allow them to rest. 6. While the meatballs are resting, heat the marinara in a saucepan on the stove over medium heat. 7. Place the courgette noodles in the air fryer, and cook at 204ºC for 3 to 5 minutes. 8. To serve, place the courgette noodles in serving bowls. Top with meatballs and warm marinara.

Turkey Mince Pasta Bake

Serves 2-3

Prep time: 5 minutes | Cook time: 20 minutes

Ingredients:

- 250g turkey minced meat
- 125g diced onions
- 1 tbsp flaxseed oil
- 1 diced yellow bell pepper
- 1/8 tsp sea salt
- 1/8 tsp ground black pepper
- 450g plain boiled pasta
- 250ml pasta sauce
- 60g grated cheddar cheese

Instructions:

1. Depending on your air fryer, select the 'scar/saute' function at medium heat or use a stove and pan

2. Start by pouring oil into the barrel of the air fryer for 3-4 minutes

3. Incorporate the onions and bell pepper for 3-4 minutes

4. Toss in the minced turkey to brown, and treacle with salt/pepper

5. Dollop the pasta sauce and stir thoroughly

6. Transfer the food content into a baking dish and sprinkle the cheddar on top

7. Now set the air fryer to 180°C. Place the baking dish in the air fryer and cook for 10-12 minutes

8. Retrieve the pasta bake and serve

Chicken and Mushroom Pie

Serves 4

Prep time: 30 minutes / Cook time: 1 hour

Ingredients

- 4 boneless chicken breasts, cut into bite-sized pieces
- 1 tbsp olive oil
- 1 large onion, chopped
- 2 cloves of garlic, minced
- 250g button mushrooms, sliced
- 2 tbsp butter
- 2 tbsp plain flour
- 250ml chicken stock
- 125ml whole milk
- 1 tsp dried thyme
- 1 sheet of ready-rolled shortcrust pastry
- 1 sheet of ready-rolled puff pastry
- 1 egg, beaten

Instructions

1. Preheat oven to 180°C fan.
2. In a large pan, heat the olive oil over high heat. Add the chicken and cook for 5 minutes until browned on all sides. Remove the chicken from the pan and set aside.
3. In the same pan, add the onions and garlic. Sauté for 5 minutes until soft and golden. Add the sliced mushrooms and butter, and sauté for 5 more minutes until the mushrooms have released their moisture and become tender.
4. Sprinkle the flour over the mushroom mixture, and stir well to combine. Gradually pour in the chicken stock and milk, stirring constantly to prevent lumps from forming. Add the thyme and season with salt and black pepper to taste. Bring to a simmer and cook for 5 minutes until the sauce has thickened.
5. Return the chicken to the pan, and stir well to coat it in the sauce. Transfer the mixture to a 23cm pie dish.
6. On a floured surface, roll out the shortcrust pastry to the thickness of a pound coin. Cut out a circle that is slightly larger than the rim of the pie dish.

Place the circle over the chicken mixture and press the edges to seal. Prick the top with a fork.

7. Roll out the puff pastry on a floured surface to the thickness of a pound coin. Cut out a circle that is slightly larger than the rim of the pie dish. Place the circle over the shortcrust pastry and press the edges to seal. Make a small hole in the center of the pie to allow steam to escape.
8. Brush the pie with beaten egg and bake in the preheated oven for 40-45 minutes or until golden brown and puffed up.
9. Remove from the oven and let it cool for a few minutes before serving. Enjoy hot!

Chicken Breasts with Asparagus and Beans

Serves: 2

Prep time: 20 minutes / Cook time: 25 minutes

Ingredients:

- 125 g canned cannellini beans, rinsed
- 1½ tablespoons red wine vinegar
- 1 garlic clove, minced
- 2 tablespoons extra-virgin olive oil, divided
- Salt and ground black pepper, to taste
- ½ red onion, sliced thinly
- 230 g asparagus, trimmed and cut into 1-inch lengths
- 2 (230 g) boneless, skinless chicken breasts, trimmed
- ¼ teaspoon paprika
- ½ teaspoon ground coriander
- 60 g baby rocket, rinsed and drained

Instructions

1. Preheat the air fryer to 204ºC.
2. Warm the beans in microwave for 1 minutes and combine with red wine vinegar, garlic, 1 tablespoon of olive oil, ¼ teaspoon of salt, and ¼ teaspoon of ground black pepper in a bowl. Stir to mix well.
3. Combine the onion with ⅛ teaspoon of salt,

⅛ teaspoon of ground black pepper, and 2 teaspoons of olive oil in a separate bowl. Toss to coat well.

4. Place the onion in the air fryer and air fry for 2 minutes, then add the asparagus and air fry for 8 more minutes or until the asparagus is tender. Shake the basket halfway through. Transfer the onion and asparagus to the bowl with beans. Set aside.

5. Toss the chicken breasts with remaining Ingredients, except for the baby arugula, in a large bowl. 6. Put the chicken breasts in the air fryer and air fry for 14 minutes or until the internal temperature of the chicken reaches at least 76°C. Flip the breasts halfway through. 7. Remove the chicken from the air fryer and serve on an aluminum foil with asparagus, beans, onion, and rocket. Sprinkle with salt and ground black pepper. Toss to serve.

Jerk chicken

Serves: 4

Prep time: 10 minutes / Cook time: 20 minutes

Ingredients:

- 4 chicken legs or thighs
- 2 tablespoons jerk seasoning
- 1 tablespoon olive oil

Instructions:

1. Preheat your air fryer to 200°C.
2. Rub the chicken with the jerk seasoning and olive oil until well coated.
3. Arrange the chicken in the air fryer basket in a single layer.
4. Cook for 10 minutes.
5. After 10 minutes, flip the chicken over and cook for another 10 minutes until cooked through and golden brown.
6. Serve the jerk chicken hot with your choice of sides, such as rice and peas, plantains, or coleslaw.

Lemon herb turkey breast

Serves: 4

Prep time: 10 minutes / Cook time: 30 minutes

Ingredients:

- 500g turkey breast
- 2 tbsp olive oil
- 1 lemon, juiced and zested
- 1 tbsp dried thyme
- 1 tbsp dried rosemary
- 1 tsp garlic powder
- 1 tsp onion powder
- Salt and pepper, to taste

Instructions:

1. Preheat the air fryer to 180°C.
2. In a small bowl, mix together the olive oil, lemon juice and zest, thyme, rosemary, garlic powder, onion powder, salt and pepper.
3. Rub the turkey breast with the herb mixture, making sure it is well coated.
4. Place the turkey breast in the air fryer basket and cook for 30 minutes, or until the internal temperature reaches 75°C.
5. Let the turkey breast rest for 5 minutes before slicing and serving.

Duck spring rolls

Serves: 8 spring rolls

Prep time: 20 minutes / Cook time: 12 minutes

Ingredients:

- 200g cooked duck meat, shredded
- 1 carrot, julienned
- 1/2 red pepper, julienned
- 2 spring onions, sliced
- 1 tbsp soy sauce
- 1 tbsp hoisin sauce
- 1 tsp sesame oil
- 8 spring roll wrappers

Instructions:

1. In a bowl, mix together the duck meat, carrot, red pepper, spring onions, soy sauce, hoisin sauce, and sesame oil.
2. Lay a spring roll wrapper on a flat surface with one corner pointing towards you.
3. Spoon 2-3 tablespoons of the filling onto the bottom third of the wrapper.
4. Roll the wrapper up over the filling, fold in the

sides, and continue rolling until the filling is completely enclosed.
5. Repeat with the remaining wrappers and filling.
6. Preheat the air fryer to 200°C.
7. Place the spring rolls in the air fryer basket and cook for 12 minutes, turning once halfway through, until golden and crispy.
8. Serve and enjoy!

Pesto chicken thighs

Serves: 2-3

Prep time: 10 minutes / Cook time: 25 minutes

Ingredients:

- 4 bone-in chicken thighs (about 600g)
- 2 tbsp pesto sauce
- 1 garlic clove, minced
- 1 tbsp olive oil
- 1/2 tsp sea salt
- 1/4 tsp ground black pepper

Instructions:

1. Pat the chicken thighs dry with paper towels.
2. In a bowl, mix together the pesto sauce, minced garlic, olive oil, salt, and black pepper.
3. Coat the chicken thighs with the pesto mixture.
4. Preheat your air fryer to 190°C for 5 minutes.
5. Arrange the chicken thighs in the air fryer basket, making sure they are not touching each other.
6. Select air fry at 190°C for 25 minutes.
7. Halfway through cooking, turn the chicken thighs over using silicone-tipped tongs.
8. Once cooked, let the chicken thighs rest for a few minutes before serving.
9. Enjoy with your favourite sides!

Curry chicken wings

Serves: 2-3

Prep time: 10 minutes / Cook time: 25 minutes

Ingredients:

- 500g chicken wings
- 2 tbsp curry powder
- 1 tsp garlic powder
- 1 tsp onion powder
- 1/2 tsp sea salt
- 1/4 tsp ground black pepper
- 1 tbsp olive oil

Instructions:

1. Pat the chicken wings dry with paper towels.
2. In a bowl, mix together the curry powder, garlic powder, onion powder, salt, and black pepper.
3. Coat the chicken wings with the spice mixture.
4. Preheat your air fryer to 190°C for 5 minutes.
5. Arrange the chicken wings in the air fryer basket, making sure they are not touching each other.
6. Select air fry at 190°C for 25 minutes.
7. Halfway through cooking, turn the chicken wings over using silicone-tipped tongs.
8. Once cooked, let the chicken wings rest for a few minutes before serving.
9. Enjoy with your favourite dipping sauce!

Honey mustard duck breast

Serves: 2

Prep time: 10 minutes / Cook time: 18 minutes

Ingredients:

- 2 duck breasts (about 300g each)
- 2 tbsp honey
- 2 tbsp Dijon mustard
- 1 tbsp olive oil
- 1/2 tsp sea salt
- 1/4 tsp ground black pepper

Instructions:

1. Pat the duck breasts dry with paper towels.
2. Score the skin of each duck breast with a sharp knife, making shallow cuts about 1 cm apart.
3. In a bowl, mix together the honey, Dijon mustard, olive oil, salt, and black pepper.
4. Brush the mixture over the duck breasts, making sure to coat the skin well.
5. Preheat your air fryer to 180°C for 5 minutes.
6. Arrange the duck breasts in the air fryer basket, skin side up.
7. Select air fry at 180°C for 18 minutes.
8. Halfway through cooking, spoon some of the honey mustard mixture over the duck breasts.
9. Once cooked, let the duck breasts rest for a few minutes before slicing and serving.
10. Enjoy with your favourite sides!

Spicy chicken skewers

Serves: 2

Prep time: 15 minutes / Cook time: 12 minutes

Ingredients:

- 350g chicken breast, cut into 2 cm cubes
- 1 red pepper, cut into 2 cm squares
- 1 green pepper, cut into 2 cm squares
- 1 red onion, cut into 2 cm squares
- 2 tbsp olive oil
- 2 tbsp smoked paprika
- 1 tsp cumin powder
- 1 tsp garlic powder
- 1 tsp salt
- 1/2 tsp black pepper
- 4 wooden skewers, soaked in water for 30 minutes

Instructions:

1. Preheat the air fryer to 200°C.
2. In a small bowl, mix together olive oil, smoked paprika, cumin powder, garlic powder, salt and black pepper to make the spice paste.
3. Thread the chicken, red and green bell peppers, and red onion onto the skewers, alternating between chicken and vegetables.
4. Brush the skewers with the spice paste on all sides.
5. Arrange the skewers on the crisper plate and spray with cooking oil.
6. Select air fry at 200°C for 12 minutes.
7. After 6 minutes, turn the skewers over using silicone-tipped tongs and spray with cooking oil on the other side. Reinsert the drawer to continue cooking.
8. Serve hot with a side of rice or salad.

Cajun turkey burgers

Serves: 2

Prep time: 10 minutes / Cook time: 12 minutes

Ingredients:

- 350g turkey mince
- 1 tsp garlic powder
- 1 tsp dried thyme
- 1 tsp smoked paprika
- 1 tsp onion powder
- 1 tsp dried oregano
- 1/2 tsp cayenne pepper
- 1/4 tsp black pepper
- 2 slices of cheese
- 4 slices of tomato
- 1/2 tsp salt
- 2 burger buns
- 4 lettuce leaves
- 4 slices of red onion

Instructions:

1. Preheat the air fryer to 200°C.
2. In a medium bowl, mix together turkey mince, smoked paprika, garlic powder, onion powder, thyme, oregano, cayenne pepper, salt and black pepper.
3. Divide the mixture into 2 portions and shape them into burger patties.
4. Arrange the patties on the crisper plate and spray with cooking oil.
5. Select air fry at 200°C for 12 minutes.
6. After 6 minutes, turn the patties over using silicone-tipped tongs and spray with cooking oil on the other side. Reinsert the drawer to continue cooking.
7. Place the burger buns on the crisper plate and toast them for the last 2 minutes of cooking.
8. Assemble the burgers with lettuce, tomato, red onion and cheese slices.
9. Serve hot with a side of sweet potato fries or coleslaw.

Lemon garlic chicken kabobs

Serves: 2

Prep time: 15 minutes / Cook time: 12 minutes

Ingredients:

- 350g chicken breast, cut into 2 cm cubes
- 1 red pepper, cut into 2 cm squares
- 1 yellow pepper, cut into 2 cm squares
- 1 red onion, cut into 2 cm squares
- 2 tbsp olive oil
- 2 garlic cloves, minced
- 1 lemon, juiced and zested
- 1 tsp dried oregano
- 1/2 tsp salt
- 1/4 tsp black pepper
- 4 wooden skewers, soaked in water for 30 minutes

Instructions:

1. Preheat the air fryer to 190°C.
2. In a large bowl, combine the chicken, peppers,

onion, olive oil, garlic, lemon juice and zest, oregano, salt, and black pepper. Toss to coat evenly.
3. Thread the chicken and vegetables onto the skewers, alternating between the chicken and vegetables.
4. Place the skewers in the air fryer basket in a single layer.
5. Cook for 12 minutes or until the chicken is cooked through and the vegetables are tender, flipping the skewers halfway through.
6. Serve hot and enjoy!

Jamaican-style curry turkey legs

Serves: 4

Prep time: 10 minutes / Cook time: 30 minutes

Ingredients:

- 4 turkey legs
- 2 tbsp Jamaican curry powder
- 1 tsp garlic powder
- 1 tsp onion powder
- 1 tsp dried thyme
- 1 tsp ground allspice
- 1/2 tsp cayenne pepper
- 1 tsp sea salt
- 1/4 tsp black pepper
- 2 tbsp olive oil

Instructions:

1. In a small bowl, mix together the Jamaican curry powder, garlic powder, onion powder, dried thyme, ground allspice, cayenne pepper, sea salt, and black pepper.
2. Rub the spice mixture all over the turkey legs, coating them evenly.
3. Drizzle with olive oil.
4. Select air fry and cook at 200°C for 15 minutes.
5. Using silicone tipped tongs, turn your turkey legs and return to the air fryer basket for a further 15 minutes.
6. Serve hot with your favourite sides.

Peri peri chicken thighs

Serves: 4

Prep time: 10 minutes / Cook time: 25 minutes

Ingredients:

- 8 bone-in chicken thighs
- 4 tbsp peri peri sauce
- 1 tsp garlic powder
- 1 tsp paprika
- 1/2 tsp sea salt
- 1/4 tsp black pepper
- 2 tbsp olive oil

Instructions:

1. In a small bowl, mix together the peri peri sauce, garlic powder, paprika, sea salt, and black pepper.
2. Brush the chicken thighs with the mixture, coating them evenly.
3. Drizzle with olive oil.
4. Select air fry at 200°C for 10 minutes.
5. After 5 minutes, turn the chicken thighs over using silicone-tipped tongs and brush them with cooking oil on the other side.
6. Reinsert the drawer to continue cooking.
7. Serve hot with your favourite sides.

Cranberry stuffed turkey meatloaf

Serves: 4-6

Prep time: 20 minutes / Cook time: 35 minutes

Ingredients:

- 500g turkey mince
- 60g breadcrumbs
- 60ml milk
- 1 egg
- 1 tsp dried sage
- 1/2 tsp sea salt
- 1/4 tsp black pepper
- 40g dried cranberries
- 2 tbsp olive oil

Instructions:

1. In a large bowl, mix together the turkey mince, breadcrumbs, milk, egg, dried sage, sea salt, and black pepper until well combined.
2. Press the mixture into the air fryer basket, forming a well in the centre.

3. Fill the well with dried cranberries.
4. Cover with the remaining turkey mixture, pressing it down gently to seal.
5. Drizzle with olive oil.
6. Select air fry at 180°C for 20 minutes.
7. Use a silicone-tipped tong to carefully turn the meatloaf over.
8. Air fry for 10 minutes then, remove the meatloaf from the air fryer and let it rest for 5 minutes before slicing and serving.
9. Enjoy your delicious cranberry stuffed turkey meatloaf!

Lemon-Pepper Chicken Drumsticks

Serves:2

Prep time: 30 minutes / Cook time: 30 minutes

Ingredients:

- 2 teaspoons freshly ground coarse black pepper
- 1 teaspoon baking powder
- ½ teaspoon garlic powder
- 4 chicken drumsticks (115 g each)
- Kosher or coarse sea salt, to taste
- 1 lemon

Instructions:

1. In a small bowl, stir together the pepper, baking powder, and garlic powder. Place the drumsticks on a plate and sprinkle evenly with the baking powder mixture, turning the drumsticks so they're well coated. Let the drumsticks stand in the refrigerator for at least 1 hour or up to overnight.
2. Sprinkle the drumsticks with salt, then transfer them to the air fryer, standing them bone-end up and leaning against the wall of the air fryer basket. Air fry at 192°C until cooked through and crisp on the outside, about 30 minutes.
3. Transfer the drumsticks to a serving platter and finely grate the zest of the lemon over them while they're hot. Cut the lemon into wedges and serve with the warm drumsticks.

Chicken and Vegetable Curry

Serves:2

Prep time: 10 minutes / Cook time: 24 minutes

Ingredients

- 200g Chicken thigh cut into small pieces
- 1 Red onion, chopped
- 1 Red pepper, finely chopped
- 1 Courgette, chopped
- 2 Cloves Garlic, crushed
- 2cm fresh Red chilli, finely grated
- 2cm fresh Ginger, finely grated
- 1 teaspoon Olive Oil
- 1 teaspoon Cumin
- 1 teaspoon Curry Powder
- 1 teaspoon Turmeric
- 1 tin 400g Chopped Tomato's
- 1 teaspoon Honey
- 2 teaspoon Almond Butter
- Salt and pepper
- 2 Handfuls of fresh Spinach
- To serve:
- 2 Tablespoons Greek Yoghurt
- 2 portions of Pilau Rice, cooked
- Some chopped Coriander

Instructions:

1. In an oven friendly bowl such as a 20cm cake tin with high sides add all the Ingredients except the Spinach and mix well together.
2. Switch the Air Fryer on and set it for 20 minutes at 190°c. Add the bowl to the air fryer pan.
3. Cook for 10 minutes. After the 10 minutes open the air fryer and stir the Ingredients well. Close the lid and cook for the remaining 10 minutes. After it has finished reset the air fryer for 180°c for 4 minutes. Add the Spinach and stir well. Cook for 2 minutes, open and stir and then cook for the remaining 2 minutes.
4. Once the chicken curry is cooked stir in the Yoghurt and Coriander and serve over the rice.

Peanut Butter Chicken Salad

Serves:2

Prep time: 5 minutes / Cook time: 18 minutes

Ingredients

- 2 Chicken breasts (around 120g each)
- 1 teaspoon Olive Oil
- 1 teaspoon Paprika
- Salt and Pepper
- ½ large Cucumber
- 2 large Carrots
- 2 large handfuls of salad leaves
- ½ Avocado sliced
- Dressing:
- 2 teaspoons Crunchy Peanut Butter
- 20ml teaspoons Soya Sauce
- 20ml teaspoons Sesame Oil
- 20ml of freshly squeezed lime juice

Instructions:

1. Wash Chicken breasts and pat dry with kitchen towel. Drizzle with Olive Oil, Paprika, salt and pepper.
2. Switch the Air Fryer on and set it for 18 minutes at 190°c. Add the chicken to the air fryer pan. Close the lid and cook for 18 minutes.
3. While cooking shave the carrots and cucumber into ribbons and mix with the salad leaves and Avocado. Mix the dressing Ingredients together in a separate small bowl.
4. Once chicken is cooked, remove from the air fryer and place over the salad. Drizzle over the dressing to serve.

Air Fryer Stuffed Chicken Breast with Spinach and Feta

Serves:4

Prep time: 15 minutes / Cook time: 18-20 minutes

Ingredients

- 4 boneless, skinless chicken breasts (approx. 120 g each)
- 100 g fresh spinach leaves, chopped
- 100 g crumbled feta cheese
- 1 clove garlic, minced
- 2 tbsp olive oil
- Salt and pepper, to taste
- 1 lemon, zested and juiced
- 2 tbsp all-purpose flour
- 2 tbsp Panko breadcrumbs
- 1 egg, beaten

Instructions:

1. Preheat the air fryer to 200°C.
2. In a bowl, mix together the chopped spinach, feta cheese, garlic, 1 tablespoon of the olive oil, salt, pepper, and lemon zest.
3. Use a sharp knife to make a pocket in the side of each chicken breast. Spoon the spinach mixture into each pocket, and secure with toothpicks.
4. In a shallow dish, mix together the flour, salt, pepper, and lemon juice.
5. In another shallow dish, place the beaten egg.
6. In a third shallow dish, place the Panko breadcrumbs.
7. Dip each chicken breast into the flour mixture, then the egg mixture, and finally the Panko mixture, making sure it is well coated.
8. Place the chicken breasts in a single layer in the air fryer basket.
9. Brush the remaining olive oil over the chicken.
10. Cook the chicken for 18-20 minutes, turning it halfway through cooking, until the internal temperature reaches 165°F (74°C) and the chicken is crispy and golden brown.
11. Serve the chicken with a side of the honey mustard dip. Enjoy!

Tandoori Chicken

Serves:4

Prep time: 30 minutes / Cook time: 15-20 minutes

Ingredients

- 4 boneless chicken breasts
- 480 g plain yogurt
- 2 tablespoons of tandoori masala
- 2 cloves of garlic, minced
- Salt and pepper, to taste
- Oil, for brushing

Instructions:

1. Preheat the air fryer to 180 °C.

2. In a small bowl, mix together the yogurt, tandoori masala, minced garlic, salt, and pepper.
3. Place the chicken breasts in a large resealable bag and pour the tandoori yogurt mixture over them. Seal the bag and toss to coat the chicken. Marinate for at least 30 minutes or overnight in the refrigerator.
4. Brush the chicken with a little oil and place them in the air fryer.
5. Cook for 15-20 minutes, or until the chicken is cooked through and the coating is golden brown

20 Chicken Croquettes with Creole Sauce

Serves:4

Prep time: 30 minutes / Cook time: 10 minutes

Ingredients

- 280 g shredded cooked chicken
- 120 g shredded Cheddar cheese
- 2 eggs
- 15 g finely chopped onion
- 25 g almond meal
- 1 tablespoon poultry seasoning
- Olive oil
- Creole Sauce:
- 60 g mayonnaise
- 60 g sour cream
- 1½ teaspoons Dijon mustard
- 1½ teaspoons fresh lemon juice
- ½ teaspoon garlic powder
- ½ teaspoon Creole seasoning

Instructions:

1. In a large bowl, combine the chicken, Cheddar, eggs, onion, almond meal, and poultry seasoning. Stir gently until thoroughly combined. Cover and refrigerate for 30 minutes.
2. Meanwhile, to make the Creole sauce: In a small bowl, whisk together the mayonnaise, sour cream, Dijon mustard, lemon juice, garlic powder, and Creole seasoning until thoroughly combined. Cover and refrigerate until ready to serve.
3. Preheat the air fryer to 200ºC. Divide the chicken

mixture into 8 portions and shape into patties.
4. Working in batches if necessary, arrange the patties in a single layer in the air fryer basket and coat both sides lightly with olive oil. Pausing halfway through the cooking time to flip the patties, air fry for 10 minutes, or until lightly browned and the cheese is melted. Serve with the Creole sauce.

Nacho Chicken Fries

Serves:4-6

Prep time: 20 minutes / Cook time: 6-7 minutes

Ingredients

- 450 g chicken tenders
- Salt, to taste
- 30 g flour
- 2 eggs
- 90 g panko bread crumbs
- 20 g crushed organic nacho cheese tortilla chips
- Oil for misting or cooking spray
- Seasoning Mix:
- 1 tablespoon chili powder
- 1 teaspoon ground cumin
- ½ teaspoon garlic powder
- ½ teaspoon onion powder

Instructions:

1. Stir together all seasonings in a small cup and set aside.
2. Cut chicken tenders in half crosswise, then cut into strips no wider than about ½ inch.
3. Preheat the air fryer to 200ºC.
4. Salt chicken to taste. Place strips in large bowl and sprinkle with 1 tablespoon of the seasoning mix. Stir well to distribute seasonings.
5. Add flour to chicken and stir well to coat all sides. 6. Beat eggs together in a shallow dish. 7. In a second shallow dish, combine the panko, crushed chips, and the remaining 2 teaspoons of seasoning mix. 8. Dip chicken strips in eggs, then roll in crumbs. Mist with oil or cooking spray. 9. Chicken strips will cook best if done in two batches. They can be crowded and overlapping a little but not stacked in double or triple layers. 10. Cook for 4 minutes. Shake basket, mist with

oil, and cook 2 to 3 more minutes, until chicken juices run clear and outside is crispy. 11. Repeat step 10 to cook remaining chicken fries.

Air Fried Chicken Wings with BBQ Sauce

Serves:4

Prep time: 10 minutes / Cook time: 25 minutes

Ingredients

- 1 kg chicken wings
- 1 tsp garlic powder
- 1 tsp onion powder
- 1 tsp paprika
- 1/2 tsp cayenne pepper
- Salt and black pepper to taste
- 1/2 cup all-purpose flour
- 2 tbsp olive oil
- 1/2 cup BBQ sauce

Instructions

1. In a large mixing bowl, toss the chicken wings with garlic powder, onion powder, paprika, cayenne pepper, salt, and black pepper. Add the flour and toss again until the chicken wings are coated.
2. Preheat the air fryer to 375°F (190°C) for 5 minutes.
3. Arrange the chicken wings on the air fryer basket, leaving space between them. Brush with olive oil.
4. Air fry for 20-25 minutes or until the chicken wings are crispy and cooked through, flipping halfway through.
5. Brush the chicken wings with BBQ sauce and air fry for an additional 2-3 minutes or until the sauce is hot and bubbly.
6. Serve hot with additional BBQ sauce and your favorite sides.

Air Fried Tandoori Chicken

Serves:4

Prep time: 10 minutes / Cook time: 20 minutes

Ingredients

- 4 bone-in chicken thighs, skin removed
- 1 cup plain Greek yogurt
- 2 tbsp tandoori spice blend
- 2 tbsp lemon juice
- 1 tsp ground cumin
- 1 tsp ground coriander
- 1/2 tsp ground ginger
- 1/2 tsp sea salt
- 1/4 tsp ground black pepper

Instructions

1. In a large bowl, whisk together the yogurt, tandoori spice blend, lemon juice, cumin, coriander, ginger, sea salt, and black pepper.
2. Add the chicken thighs to the bowl and toss to coat them in the marinade.
3. Cover the bowl with plastic wrap and refrigerate for at least 1 hour, or up to overnight.
4. Preheat the air fryer to 200°C for 5 minutes.
5. Remove the chicken thighs from the marinade and shake off any excess. Place them in the air fryer basket in a single layer.
6. Select "AIR FRY" at 200°C for 20 minutes. Select the "START/STOP" button to begin cooking. When the timer reaches 10 minutes, open the air fryer and turn the chicken thighs over using silicone-tipped tongs.
7. Close the air fryer and continue cooking until the timer is up.
8. Remove the chicken thighs from the air fryer and let them rest for 5 minutes before serving.

Chapter 5: Fish and Seafood

Air fryer blackened salmon

Serves: 2

Prep time: 10 minutes / Cook time: 12 minutes

Ingredients:

- 2 salmon fillets, skin-on (approx. 150g each)
- 1 tsp paprika
- 1/2 tsp onion powder
- 1/2 tsp garlic powder
- 1/4 tsp cayenne pepper
- 1/2 tsp dried thyme
- 1/2 tsp dried oregano
- 1/4 tsp sea salt
- 1/4 tsp black pepper
- 1 tbsp olive oil

Instructions:

1. Preheat the air fryer to 200°C for 5 minutes.
2. In a small bowl, mix together the paprika, onion powder, garlic powder, cayenne pepper, thyme, oregano, sea salt, and black pepper.
3. Rub the spice mixture over both sides of the salmon fillets.
4. Drizzle olive oil over the fillets.
5. Place the fillets skin-side down in the air fryer basket.
6. Select air fry at 200°C for 6 minutes.
7. Using silicone tipped tongs, turn your salmon and continue to fry for a further 6 minutes.
8. Remove from the fryer and serve hot!

Spicy shrimp skewers

Serves: 2

Prep time: 10 minutes / Cook time: 8 minutes

Ingredients:

- 16 large raw shrimp, peeled and deveined
- 1 tbsp olive oil
- 1 tbsp lemon juice
- 1/2 tsp paprika
- 1/2 tsp garlic powder
- 1/4 tsp cayenne pepper
- 1/4 tsp sea salt
- 1/4 tsp black pepper
- 8 skewers

Instructions:

1. Preheat the air fryer to 200°C for 5 minutes.
2. In a small bowl, mix together the olive oil, lemon juice, paprika, garlic powder, cayenne pepper, sea salt, and black pepper.
3. Thread four shrimp onto each skewer.
4. Brush the shrimp skewers with the spice mixture, making sure they are well coated.
5. Place the skewers in the air fryer basket.
6. Select air fry at 200°C for 4 minutes. Turn the skewers over and cook for a further 4 minutes on the other side.
7. Serve and enjoy!

Crispy fried squid rings

Serves: 4

Prep time: 20 minutes / Cook time: 10 minutes

Ingredients:

- 400g squid rings
- 120g all-purpose flour
- 1 tsp smoked paprika
- 1/2 tsp garlic powder
- 1/4 tsp cayenne pepper
- 1/4 tsp sea salt
- 1/4 tsp black pepper
- 1 egg, beaten
- 250g panko breadcrumbs

Instructions:

1. Preheat the air fryer to 200°C for 5 minutes.
2. In a shallow dish, mix together the flour, smoked paprika, garlic powder, cayenne pepper, sea salt, and black pepper.
3. In a separate shallow dish, beat the egg.
4. In a third shallow dish, place the panko breadcrumbs.
5. Dip each squid ring first into the flour mixture, then into the egg, and finally into the panko

breadcrumbs, making sure it is well coated.

6. Place the coated squid rings in the air fryer basket.
7. Select air fry at 200°C for 5 minutes. Turn the squid rings over and cook for a further 5 minutes on the other side.
8. Serve the crispy fried squid rings with lemon wedges and tartar sauce.

Seafood stuffed mushrooms

Serves: 4

Prep time: 15 minutes / Cook time: 12 minutes

Ingredients:

- 8 large mushrooms
- 100g cooked prawns, chopped
- 100g canned crab meat, drained and flaked
- 1 small onion, finely chopped
- 1 garlic clove, minced
- 1 tbsp olive oil
- 1/4 tsp dried oregano
- 1/4 tsp dried thyme
- 1/4 tsp paprika
- 1/4 tsp sea salt
- 1/4 tsp black pepper
- 50g grated parmesan cheese

Instructions:

1. Remove the stems from the mushrooms and chop them finely.
2. In a skillet, heat the olive oil over medium heat.
3. Add the onion and garlic and sauté until the onion is translucent.
4. Add the chopped mushroom stems and cook for another 3 minutes.
5. Add the prawns, crab meat, oregano, thyme, paprika, sea salt, and black pepper to the skillet and cook for an additional 2 minutes.
6. Preheat the air fryer to 180°C.
7. Stuff the mushroom caps with the seafood mixture and place them on the crisper plate.
8. Sprinkle the grated parmesan cheese over the stuffed mushrooms.
9. Select air fry at 180°C for 6 minutes.
10. Turn and cook for another 6 minutes.
11. Serve hot and enjoy!

Scallop and bacon bites

Serves: 4

Prep time: 10 minutes / Cook time: 10 minutes

Ingredients:

- 8 large scallops, cleaned and trimmed
- 4 rashers of streaky bacon, cut into halves
- 1 tbsp olive oil
- 1 tbsp honey
- 1 tbsp soy sauce
- 1 tbsp lemon juice
- 1/2 tsp garlic powder
- 1/4 tsp sea salt
- 1/4 tsp black pepper

Instructions:

1. In a bowl, whisk together the olive oil, honey, soy sauce, lemon juice, garlic powder, sea salt, and black pepper.
2. Add the scallops to the bowl and marinate for 10 minutes.
3. Wrap each scallop with a half slice of bacon, securing it with a toothpick.
4. Place the bacon-wrapped scallops on the crisper plate.
5. Preheat the air fryer to 200°C.
6. Select air fry at 200°C for 5 minutes.
7. Turn the bites over and air fry at 200°C for another 5 minutes.
8. Serve hot and enjoy!

Teriyaki glazed salmon skewers

Serves: 4

Prep time: 10 minutes / Cook time: 12 minutes

Ingredients:

- 4 salmon fillets, skin removed, cut into 2cm cubes
- 1 red pepper, cut into 2cm pieces
- 1 green pepper, cut into 2cm pieces
- 1 onion, cut into 2cm pieces
- 60ml teriyaki sauce
- 1 tbsp honey
- 1 tbsp olive oil
- 1 tsp sesame oil

- 1 garlic clove, minced
- 1/4 tsp sea salt
- 1/4 tsp black pepper
- 4 skewers

Instructions:

1. Soak the skewers in water for 30 minutes.
2. In a small saucepan, combine soy sauce, brown sugar, mirin, rice vinegar, ginger, and garlic. Cook over medium heat until sugar dissolves and sauce thickens, about 5 minutes.
3. In a small bowl, whisk together cornstarch and water until smooth. Add to the saucepan and whisk to combine. Cook for another minute or until the sauce has thickened. Remove from heat and let cool.
4. Thread salmon cubes onto skewers and place them on the crisper plate. Brush the salmon with teriyaki sauce.
5. Select air fry at 180°C for 5 minutes.
6. When the timer goes off, remove the salmon skewers from the air fryer and brush with additional teriyaki sauce.
7. Sprinkle with sesame seeds (optional) and serve.

Coconut shrimp

Serves: 2

Prep time: 15 minutes / Cook time: 8 minutes

Ingredients:

- 12 large raw shrimp, peeled and deveined
- 120g shredded coconut
- 60g all-purpose flour
- 1 tsp garlic powder
- 1/2 tsp salt
- 1/4 tsp black pepper
- 1 large egg, beaten
- 2 tsp olive oil

Instructions:

1. In a shallow dish, mix together the shredded coconut, flour, garlic powder, salt, and black pepper.
2. Dip each shrimp in the beaten egg, then coat in the coconut mixture.
3. Preheat the air fryer to 200°C for 3 minutes.

4. Arrange the shrimp on the crisper plate and spray with olive oil.
5. Select air fry at 200°C for 8 minutes.
6. When the time is up, remove the shrimp from the air fryer and serve immediately.

Grilled sardines

Serves: 2

Prep time: 10 minutes / Cook time: 6 minutes

Ingredients:

- 4 whole sardines, gutted and scaled
- 1 lemon, cut into wedges
- 2 tbsp olive oil
- 1 tsp dried oregano
- Salt and black pepper, to taste

Instructions:

1. Preheat the air fryer to 200°C for 3 minutes.
2. In a small bowl, mix together the olive oil, oregano, salt, and black pepper.
3. Brush the mixture onto both sides of the sardines.
4. Arrange the sardines on the crisper plate and spray with olive oil.
5. Select air fry at 200°C for 6 minutes.
6. When the time is up, remove the sardines from the air fryer.
7. Serve with lemon wedges.

Cajun-style tilapia

Serves: 2

Prep time: 15 minutes / Cook time: 16 minutes

Ingredients:

- 2 (170g each) tilapia fillets
- 1 tsp Cajun seasoning
- 1/2 tsp garlic powder
- 1/2 tsp onion powder
- 1/4 tsp paprika
- 1/4 tsp dried thyme
- 1/4 tsp salt
- 1/4 tsp black pepper
- 1 tbsp olive oil

Instructions:

1. Preheat the air fryer to 200°C for 3 minutes.
2. In a small bowl, mix together the Cajun seasoning, garlic powder, onion powder, paprika, thyme, salt, and black pepper.
3. Rub the mixture onto both sides of the tilapia fillets.
4. Arrange the fillets on the crisper plate and spray with olive oil.
5. Select air fry 200°C for 8 minutes.
6. When the time is up, turn the fillets over and spray with olive oil on the other side.
7. Select air fry at 200°C for another 8 minutes.
8. When the time is up, remove the fillets from the air fryer and serve immediately.

Crab cakes

Serves: 2

Prep time: 15 minutes Cook time: 15 minutes

Ingredients:

- 120g crabmeat
- 2 tbsp mayonnaise
- 2 tbsp Dijon mustard
- 1 egg, lightly beaten
- 2 tbsp finely chopped fresh parsley
- 1 tsp Worcestershire sauce
- 1/4 tsp salt
- 1/4 tsp black pepper
- 30g breadcrumbs
- 1 tsp olive oil

Instructions:

1. In a medium mixing bowl, combine crabmeat, mayonnaise, Dijon mustard, egg, parsley, Worcestershire sauce, salt, and pepper. Mix well.
2. Add breadcrumbs and mix until the mixture holds together.
3. Divide the mixture into four portions and shape into patties.
4. Spray the air fryer basket with cooking spray. Place the patties in the basket and spray with olive oil.
5. Select air fry at 200°C for 15 minutes.
6. When the cooking time is up, carefully remove

the crab cakes from the air fryer and serve hot with your favourite dipping sauce.

Lemon garlic shrimp and asparagus

Serves: 2

Prep time: 10 minutes / Cook time: 10 minutes

Ingredients:

- 200g large shrimp, peeled and deveined
- 200g asparagus, trimmed
- 1 lemon, sliced
- 2 garlic cloves, minced
- 1 tbsp olive oil
- 1/4 tsp salt
- 1/4 tsp black pepper

Instructions:

1. In a large mixing bowl, toss shrimp, asparagus, lemon slices, garlic, olive oil, salt, and pepper together until everything is well coated.
2. Spray the air fryer basket with cooking spray.
3. Place the mixture in the basket in a single layer.
4. Select air fry at 200°C for 10 minutes.
5. When the cooking time is up, carefully remove the shrimp and asparagus from the air fryer.
6. Serve hot as a side dish or over rice or pasta.

Tandoori salmon

Serves: 2

Prep time: 15 minutes / Cook time: 10 minutes

Ingredients:

- 2 salmon fillets, skin removed
- 2 tbsp plain Greek yoghurt
- 1 tbsp tandoori spice mix
- 1 tsp lemon juice
- 1/4 tsp salt
- 1/4 tsp black pepper
- 1 tbsp olive oil

Instructions:

1. In a medium mixing bowl, combine Greek

yoghurt, tandoori spice mix, lemon juice, salt, and pepper.
2. Mix well.
3. Add salmon fillets to the mixture and coat well.
4. Marinate for 10 minutes.
5. Spray the air fryer basket with cooking spray.
6. Place the salmon fillets in the basket and brush with olive oil.
7. Select air fry at 200°C for 10 minutes.
8. When the cooking time is up, carefully remove the salmon fillets from the air fryer and serve hot with a side of rice or vegetables.

Cajun shrimp and grits

Serves: 2

Prep time: 10 minutes / Cook time: 20 minutes

Ingredients:

- For the shrimp:
- 300g raw shrimp, peeled and deveined
- 1 tbsp olive oil
- 1 tbsp Cajun seasoning
- 1/4 tsp garlic powder
- 1/4 tsp onion powder
- 1/4 tsp paprika
- Sea salt and black pepper, to taste
- For the grits:
- 100g quick-cooking grits
- 500ml water
- 1/4 tsp salt
- 1 tbsp unsalted butter
- For the topping:
- 2 slices of bacon
- 2 spring onions, sliced
- 1/4 cup grated cheddar cheese

Instructions:

1. Preheat the air fryer to 180°C.
2. In a mixing bowl, combine the shrimp with olive oil, Cajun seasoning, garlic powder, onion powder, paprika, salt, and black pepper. Mix well to coat.
3. In a saucepan, bring the water to a boil, then stir in the grits and salt. Cook for 5-7 minutes or until the grits are soft and thickened. Stir in the butter until melted and smooth.

4. Place the bacon on the air fryer rack and cook for 8-10 minutes, or until crispy. Remove and crumble.
5. Place the shrimp in the air fryer basket and cook for 6-8 minutes, or until pink and cooked through.
6. To assemble, divide the grits between two plates, top with shrimp, crumbled bacon and sliced spring onions, and grated cheddar cheese.
7. Serve immediately.

Pesto crusted sea bass

Serves: 2

Prep time: 10 minutes / Cook time: 12 minutes

Ingredients:

- 2 (170g each) sea bass fillets
- 30g panko breadcrumbs
- 20g grated parmesan cheese
- 2 tbsp pesto sauce
- 1 tbsp olive oil
- Sea salt and black pepper, to taste

Instructions:

1. Preheat the air fryer to 180°C.
2. In a small mixing bowl, combine the panko breadcrumbs, grated parmesan cheese, pesto sauce, olive oil, salt, and black pepper. Mix well.
3. Season the sea bass fillets with salt and black pepper, then coat with the pesto mixture.
4. Place the fillets in the air fryer basket and cook for 10-12 minutes, or until the crust is golden brown and the fish is cooked through.
5. Serve immediately with a side salad or roasted vegetables.

Miso glazed cod

Serves: 2

Prep time: 10 minutes / Cook time: 12 minutes

Ingredients:

- 2 (170g each) cod fillets
- 2 tbsp white miso paste
- 1 tbsp honey

- 1 tbsp rice vinegar
- 1 tbsp soy sauce
- 1 tsp sesame oil
- 1 garlic clove, minced
- 1 tsp grated ginger
- 1 spring onion, sliced

Instructions:

1. Preheat the air fryer to 180°C.
2. In a mixing bowl, combine the miso paste, honey, rice vinegar, soy sauce, sesame oil, minced garlic, and grated ginger. Mix well.
3. Season the cod fillets with salt and black pepper, then coat with the miso glaze.
4. Place the fillets in the air fryer basket and cook for 10-12 minutes, or until the fish is cooked through.
5. Serve immediately, topped with sliced spring onions.
6. Optional: serve with steamed rice or sautéed vegetables.

COD TRAYBAKE

Serves: 2

Prep time: 10 minutes / Cook time: 18 minutes

Ingredients:

- 2 Cod fillets (about 120g each)
- 200g Tenderstem broccoli
- 100g Green Beans, washed and ends cut off
- 1 medium Sweet Potato, washed and chopped
- 1 Red onion, chopped
- 1 Red pepper, washed and chopped
- Dressing:
- 60ml Sesame oil
- 1 teaspoon Miso Paste
- 1 tablespoon freshly squeezed lemon juice
- Crushed clove Garlic

Instructions:

1. Wash the fish and pat dry with some kitchen roll.
2. Whisk the dressing in a bowl.
3. Paint half the dressing over the fish fillets.
4. Switch the Air Fryer on and set it for 18 minutes at 190°c. Add the sweet potato, red onion, and red pepper to the air fryer pot and cook for 8

minutes.
5. After 8 minutes open the air fryer and add the broccoli and green beans. Mix well together and lay the fish on top. Close the lid and cook for the further 10 minutes.
6. Place the vegetables in a dish and pour over the remaining dressing. Place the fish on top and serve.

Air Fryer Garlic Butter Shrimp Scampi

Serves: 4

Prep time: 10 minutes / Cook time: 8-10 minutes

Ingredients:

- 600 g large raw shrimp, peeled and deveined
- 4 tablespoons unsalted butter, melted
- 4 cloves garlic, minced
- 2 tablespoons lemon juice
- 2 tablespoons parsley, chopped
- Salt and pepper, to taste
- 30g breadcrumbs

Instructions:

1. In a large bowl, mix together the melted butter, minced garlic, lemon juice, parsley, salt, and pepper.
2. Add the shrimp to the mixture and stir until evenly coated.
3. In a separate bowl, mix together the breadcrumbs and a pinch of salt.
4. Dip each shrimp into the breadcrumb mixture, pressing gently to adhere the breadcrumbs to the shrimp.
5. Place the breaded shrimp in a single layer in the air fryer basket.
6. Air fry at 400°F (204°C) for 8-10 minutes or until the shrimp are crispy and cooked through.
7. Serve the air fryer garlic butter shrimp scampi with some lemon wedges and additional parsley on top. Enjoy!

Tuna with Roasted Garlic and Hazelnuts

Serves: 4

Prep time: 10 minutes / Cook time: 10 minutes

Ingredients:

- 75ml of the stock from the hake
- 200g tuna fillet, cut into 1 inch x 1/2 inch pieces
- 20g hazelnuts, chopped
- 15g roasted and crushed garlic clove

Instructions:

1. Combine all of the stock Ingredients in a bowl, making sure to whisk in the hake slice at the end. Set aside for 5 minutes to allow the flavours to amalgamate.
2. Preheat your air fryer to 370 degrees.
3. Skewer the fish and roast in the air fryer.
4. Remove the hake from the stock and reserve the stock to make a sauce or to drizzle over your food.
5. Mix the roasted garlic and hazelnuts in a small bowl until well incorporated and set aside (be careful not to incorporate too much red pepper as this could alter the flavour).
6. Place the tuna on a plate and serve with brown rice, fresh salad, and roasted garlic hazelnuts.

Stuffed Sole Florentine

Serves: 4

Prep time: 10 minutes / Cook time: 25 minutes

Ingredients:

- 40 g pine nuts
- 2 tablespoons olive oil
- 90 g chopped tomatoes
- 170 g bag spinach, coarsely chopped
- 2 cloves garlic, chopped
- Salt and freshly ground black pepper, to taste
- 2 tablespoons unsalted butter, divided
- 4 Sole fillets (about 680 g)
- Dash of paprika
- ½ lemon, sliced into 4 wedges

Instructions:

1. Place the pine nuts in a baking dish that fits in your air fryer. Set the air fryer to 204ºC and air fry for 4 minutes until the nuts are lightly browned and fragrant. Remove the baking dish from the air fryer, tip the nuts onto a plate to cool, and continue preheating the air fryer. When the nuts are cool enough to handle, chop them into fine pieces.
2. In the baking dish, combine the oil, tomatoes, spinach, and garlic. Use tongs to toss until thoroughly combined. Air fry for 5 minutes until the tomatoes are softened and the spinach is wilted.
3. Transfer the vegetables to a bowl and stir in the toasted pine nuts. Season to taste with salt and freshly ground black pepper.
4. Place 1 tablespoon of the butter in the bottom of the baking dish. Lower the heat on the air fryer to 176ºC.
5. Place the sole on a clean work surface. Sprinkle both sides with salt and black pepper. Divide the vegetable mixture among the sole fillets and carefully roll up, securing with toothpicks.
6. Working in batches if necessary, arrange the fillets seam-side down in the baking dish along with 1 tablespoon of water. Top the fillets with remaining 1 tablespoon butter and sprinkle with a dash of paprika. 7.Cover loosely with foil and air fry for 10 to 15 minutes until the fish is opaque and flakes easily with a fork. Remove the toothpicks before serving with the lemon wedges.

20 FISH KEBABS

Serves: 2

Prep time: 10 minutes +1 hour for marinade / Cook time: 25 minutes

Ingredients

- 2 x 150g White fish fillets cut into large chunks
- 1 Red Onion cut into chunks
- 150g Brown Mushrooms cut into chunks
- Dressing:
- 1 Tablespoon Olive Oil

- Juice and zest of 1 lemon (reserve some juice for serving)
- Small bunch of Parsley, finely chopped
- 2 clove Garlic, crushed
- Salt and pepper
- Serve with:
- Fresh greens salad

Instructions:

1. Lay 2 wooden skewers in some cold water to soak.
2. In a mixing bowl add the fish, vegetables and dressing Ingredients and mix well together. Allow to marinade for 1 hour before cooking.
3. Load the skewers, alternating between fish, onion and mushrooms.
4. Switch the Air Fryer on and set it for 10 minutes at 200°c. Add the skewers to the Air Fryer basket and cook for 10 minutes.
5. Once the fish is cooked, serve with the salad and squeeze over some lemon juice.

Smoky Prawns and Chorizo Tapas

Serves: 2-4

Prep time: 15 minutes / Cook time: 10 minutes

Ingredients

- 110 g Spanish (cured) chorizo, halved horizontally and sliced crosswise
- 230 g raw medium prawns, peeled and deveined
- 1 tablespoon extra-virgin olive oil
- 1 small shallot, halved and thinly sliced
- 1 garlic clove, minced
- 1 tablespoon finely chopped fresh oregano
- ½ teaspoon smoked Spanish paprika
- ¼ teaspoon kosher or coarse sea salt
- ¼ teaspoon black pepper
- 3 tablespoons fresh orange juice
- 1 tablespoon minced fresh parsley

Instructions:

1. Place the chorizo in a baking pan. Set the pan in the air fryer basket. Set the air fryer to 192°C for 5 minutes, or until the chorizo has started to brown and render its fat.
2. Meanwhile, in a large bowl, combine the prawns, olive oil, shallot, garlic, oregano, paprika, salt, and pepper. Toss until the prawns are well coated.
3. Transfer the prawns to the pan with the chorizo. Stir to combine. Place the pan in the air fryer basket. Cook for 10 minutes, stirring halfway through the cooking time.
4. Transfer the prawns and chorizo to a serving dish. Drizzle with the orange juice and toss to combine. Sprinkle with the parsley.

Air Fryer Cajun Shrimp Po' Boys

Serves: 4

Prep time: 10 minutes / Cook time: 8-10 minutes

Ingredients

- 500 g raw peeled and deveined shrimp
- 60 g all-purpose flour
- 30g cornmeal
- 2 tsp Cajun seasoning
- Salt and pepper, to taste
- 2 large eggs
- 60ml buttermilk
- 2-4 tbsp oil or cooking spray
- 4 large soft sub rolls
- Optional toppings: lettuce, tomato, pickles, hot sauce, and aioli or mayo

Instructions:

1. In a shallow bowl, combine the flour, cornmeal, Cajun seasoning, salt, and pepper.
2. In another shallow bowl, whisk together the eggs and buttermilk.
3. Dip each shrimp into the egg mixture, then coat in the flour mixture, pressing to adhere.
4. Preheat the air fryer to 380°F (190°C) for 5 minutes.
5. Grease the air fryer basket with oil or cooking spray.
6. Place the coated shrimp in the air fryer basket in a single layer.
7. Cook for 6-8 minutes, or until crispy and golden

brown, flipping halfway through.

8. While the shrimp is cooking, split the sub rolls and lightly toast them in the air fryer for 1-2 minutes.

9. Serve the shrimp on the toasted sub rolls and top with your desired toppings. Serve immediately.

10. Enjoy your delicious and crispy Cajun Shrimp Po' Boys, made in the air fryer!

Cod Tacos with Mango Salsa

Serves: 4

Prep time: 15 minutes / Cook time: 17 minutes

Ingredients

- 1 mango, peeled and diced
- 1 small jalapeño pepper, diced
- ½ red bell pepper, diced
- ½ red onion, minced
- Pinch chopped fresh cilantro
- Juice of ½ lime
- ¼ teaspoon salt
- ¼ teaspoon ground black pepper
- 120 ml Mexican beer
- 1 egg
- 75 g cornflour
- 90 g plain flour
- ½ teaspoon ground cumin
- ¼ teaspoon chilli powder
- 455 g cod, cut into 4 pieces
- Olive oil spray
- 4 corn tortillas, or flour tortillas, at room temperature

Instructions:

1. In a small bowl, stir together the mango, jalapeño, red bell pepper, red onion, cilantro, lime juice, salt, and pepper. Set aside.

2. In a medium bowl, whisk the beer and egg.

3. In another medium bowl, stir together the cornflour, flour, cumin, and chilli powder.

4. Insert the crisper plate into the basket and the basket into the unit. Preheat the unit to 192°C.

5. Dip the fish pieces into the egg mixture and in the flour mixture to coat completely.

6. Once the unit is preheated, place a baking paper liner into the basket. Place the fish on the liner in a single layer.

7. Cook for about 9 minutes, spray the fish with olive oil. Reinsert the basket to resume cooking.

8. When the cooking is complete, the fish should be golden and crispy. Place the pieces in the tortillas, top with the mango salsa, and serve.

Air Fried Shrimp Skewers with Lemon Garlic Butter

Serves 4

Prep time: 15 minutes / Cook time: 6 minutes

Ingredients

- 500g large shrimp, peeled and deveined
- 1 lemon, cut into wedges
- 2 garlic cloves, peeled and minced
- 2 tbsp unsalted butter, melted
- 1/2 tsp sea salt
- 1/4 tsp ground black pepper
- 8 wooden skewers, soaked in water for 30 minutes

Instructions

1. Preheat the air fryer to 200°C for 5 minutes.

2. In a large bowl, toss together the shrimp, minced garlic, melted butter, sea salt, and black pepper.

3. Thread the shrimp onto the wooden skewers, making sure they are evenly distributed.

4. Place the skewers in the air fryer basket and select "AIR FRY" at 200°C for 6 minutes. Select the "START/STOP" button to begin cooking.

5. When the timer reaches 3 minutes, open the air fryer and turn the shrimp skewers over using silicone-tipped tongs.

6. Close the air fryer and continue cooking until the timer is up.

7. Remove the shrimp skewers from the air fryer and squeeze lemon wedges over them before serving. Bon appétit!

Roast beef and Yorkshire Pudding

Cook time: 20-30 minutes.

Ingredients:

For the beef:

- 1 (3-4 pound) beef roast
- 2 teaspoons kosher salt
- 1 teaspoon black pepper
- 2 tablespoons olive oil
- 2 cloves garlic, minced
- 1 teaspoon dried thyme
- 1 teaspoon dried rosemary
- For the Yorkshire pudding:
- 1 cup all-purpose flour
- 1/2 teaspoon kosher salt
- 1 cup whole milk
- 2 large eggs, beaten
- 2 tablespoons beef drippings or vegetable oil

Preparation Instructions:

1. Preheat your air fryer to 450°F (230°C).
2. Season the beef roast with salt and pepper on all sides.
3. In a small bowl, mix together the olive oil, garlic, thyme, and rosemary. Rub the herb mixture all over the beef.
4. Place the beef in a roasting pan and roast for 15 minutes. Reduce the oven temperature to 350°F (180°C) and continue to roast for 1 to 1 1/2 hours, or until the internal temperature reaches 135°F (57°C) for medium-rare or 145°F (63°C) for medium.
5. Remove the beef from the oven and let it rest for 10-15 minutes. While the beef is resting, make the Yorkshire pudding batter.
6. In a medium bowl, whisk together the flour and salt.
7. In a separate bowl, whisk together the milk and eggs.
8. Gradually add the milk mixture to the flour mixture, whisking until well combined.

9. Let the batter rest for at least 30 minutes. Increase the oven temperature to 450°F (230°C).
10. Pour the beef drippings or vegetable oil into a 9 x 13-inch baking dish and place it in the oven to heat up.
11. Once the oil is hot, remove the baking dish from the oven and pour in the Yorkshire pudding batter. Return the baking dish to the oven and bake for 15-20 minutes, or until the pudding is puffed and golden brown.
12. Serve the beef and Yorkshire pudding together for a classic British meal. Enjoy!

Korean-style beef skewers

Serves: 4

Prep time: 15 minutes / Cook time: 12 minutes

Ingredients:

- 500g beef sirloin, cut into thin strips
- 2 tbsp soy sauce
- 2 tbsp brown sugar
- 1 tbsp sesame oil
- 1 tbsp rice vinegar
- 1 tbsp gochujang (Korean red chilli paste)
- 1 tbsp grated fresh ginger
- 2 cloves garlic, minced
- 1 red onion, cut into bite-sized pieces
- 1 green pepper, cut into bite-sized pieces
- Bamboo skewers, soaked in water for 30 minutes
- Sea salt and ground black pepper, to taste

Instructions:

1. In a medium-sized mixing bowl, combine the soy sauce, brown sugar, sesame oil, rice vinegar, gochujang, ginger, and garlic. Stir to combine.
2. Add the beef strips to the bowl and toss until well coated. Allow the beef to marinate for at least 10 minutes, or up to 4 hours in the refrigerator.
3. Preheat your air fryer to 200°C.
4. Thread the marinated beef, red onion, and green bell pepper onto the soaked bamboo skewers.
5. Season with salt and pepper.

6. Arrange the skewers on the air fryer basket and cook for 12 minutes or until the beef is cooked through and the vegetables are tender. Turn the skewers halfway through the cooking time.
7. Serve hot and enjoy!

Jamaican jerk pork chops

Serves: 4

Prep time: 10 minutes / Cook time: 15 minutes

Ingredients:

- 4 bone-in pork chops
- 2 tbsp Jamaican jerk seasoning
- 1 tbsp olive oil
- Sea salt and ground black pepper, to taste

Instructions:

1. Preheat your air fryer to 190°C.
2. Rub the pork chops with Jamaican jerk seasoning and olive oil.
3. Season with salt and pepper.
4. Arrange the pork chops on the air fryer basket.
5. Cook for 15 minutes or until the internal temperature of the pork reaches 63°C.
6. Turn the pork chops halfway through the cooking time.
7. Remove from the air fryer and allow to rest for 5 minutes before serving.
8. Serve hot with your favourite sides and enjoy!

Mexican-style beef empanadas

Serves: 4

Prep time: 30 minutes / Cook time: 12 minutes

Ingredients:

- For the dough:
- 240g plain flour
- 1/4 tsp salt
- 60g unsalted butter, chilled and cubed
- 1 large egg, beaten
- 2-3 tbsp cold water
- For the filling:
- 200g lean minced beef
- 1/2 small onion, finely chopped
- 1 garlic clove, minced
- 1/2 tsp ground cumin
- 1/2 tsp smoked paprika
- 1/4 tsp dried oregano
- 1/4 tsp chilli powder
- 1/2 small red bell pepper, finely diced
- 1 tbsp tomato paste
- 30g pitted black olives, roughly chopped
- 1 tbsp chopped fresh coriander (optional)
- Salt and pepper, to taste
- For the egg wash:
- 1 large egg, beaten 1 tbsp milk

Instructions:

1. In a large bowl, whisk together flour and salt.
2. Add cubed butter and use your fingers to rub the butter into the flour until the mixture resembles coarse breadcrumbs.
3. Add beaten egg and 2 tbsp of cold water to the mixture and stir until the dough comes together.
4. If the dough is too dry, add another tablespoon of water.
5. Knead the dough for 1-2 minutes, then shape it into a ball and flatten it into a disc.
6. Cover with cling film and chill in the fridge for at least 30 minutes.
7. In a large frying pan, brown the minced beef over medium heat.
8. Add onion, garlic, cumin, smoked paprika, oregano, and chilli powder to the pan and cook for 2-3 minutes until fragrant.
9. Add red bell pepper to the pan and cook for another 2-3 minutes until softened.
10. Add tomato paste, olives, and coriander (if using) to the pan and stir to combine. Season with salt and pepper to taste.
11. Preheat the air fryer to 180°C.
12. On a lightly floured surface, roll out the chilled dough to 3mm thickness. Cut out 8 circles using a 12 cm pastry cutter.
13. Spoon 2 tablespoons of the beef filling onto one half of each dough circle, leaving a 1cm border around the edge
14. Brush the edges with water and fold the other half of the dough over the filling. Press the edges together to seal, then use a fork to crimp the edges.

15. Place the empanadas on a baking tray lined with parchment paper.
16. Whisk together the egg and milk to make an egg wash, then brush the empanadas with the egg wash.
17. Place the empanadas in the air fryer basket and cook for 10-12 minutes until golden brown and crisp.
18. Serve hot with your favourite salsa or guacamole.

Chinese-style beef and broccoli

Serves: 2

Prep time: 15 minutes / Cook time: 20 minutes

Ingredients:

- 300g beef sirloin, thinly sliced
- 1 tbsp cornstarch
- 1 tbsp soy sauce
- 1 tbsp oyster sauce
- 1 tbsp vegetable oil
- 1 tsp sesame oil
- 2 garlic cloves, minced
- 1 small broccoli head, cut into florets
- Salt and pepper to taste

Instructions:

1. In a bowl, combine the cornstarch, soy sauce, and oyster sauce. Add the beef slices and toss to coat.
2. Preheat the air fryer to 200°C.
3. In a frying pan, heat the vegetable oil and sesame oil over medium-high heat. Add the garlic and sauté until fragrant.
4. Add the beef to the pan and cook until browned, about 5-7 minutes.
5. Add the broccoli florets to the pan and continue cooking for an additional 5-7 minutes or until the broccoli is tender and the beef is cooked through.
6. Season with salt and pepper to taste.
7. Transfer the beef and broccoli to the air fryer basket and cook for 5-8 minutes or until crispy and golden.
8. Serve hot with steamed rice or noodles.

Moroccan spiced lamb chops

Serves: 2

Prep time: 15 minutes / Cook time: 12 minutes

Ingredients:

- 4 lamb chops
- 2 tsp ground cumin
- 2 tsp ground coriander
- 1 tsp paprika
- 1 tsp ground cinnamon
- Salt and pepper to taste
- 2 tbsp olive oil
- Lemon wedges, to serve

Instructions:

1. Preheat the air fryer to 200°C.
2. In a bowl, mix together the cumin, coriander, paprika, cinnamon, salt, and pepper.
3. Rub the spice mixture onto the lamb chops and coat evenly.
4. Drizzle olive oil over the lamb chops and rub to coat.
5. Place the lamb chops in the air fryer basket and cook for 6-8 minutes on each side or until browned and cooked through.
6. Serve hot with lemon wedges.

Stuffed pork tenderloin

Serves: 4

Prep time: 20 minutes / Cook time: 30 minutes

Ingredients:

- 500g pork tenderloin
- 2 tbsp olive oil
- 2 garlic cloves, minced
- 1 small onion, finely chopped
- 1 small red pepper, finely chopped
- 100g breadcrumbs
- 2 tbsp chopped parsley
- Salt and pepper to taste

Instructions:

1. Preheat the air fryer to 200°C.
2. In a frying pan, heat the olive oil over medium

heat. Add the garlic, onion, and red pepper and sauté until soft.

3. Add the breadcrumbs and parsley to the pan and mix well. Season with salt and pepper to taste.

4. Cut a slit lengthwise down the centre of the pork tenderloin and fill with the breadcrumb mixture.

5. Secure the opening with toothpicks or kitchen twine.

6. Place the stuffed pork tenderloin in the air fryer basket and cook for 25-30 minutes or until the internal temperature reaches 63°C.

7. Remove the toothpicks or kitchen twine before serving.

Indian-spiced beef burgers

Serves: 4

Prep time: 15 minutes / Cook time: 12 minutes

Ingredients:

- 500g lean beef mince
- 1 onion, grated
- 2 garlic cloves, minced
- 1 tsp ground cumin
- 1 tsp ground coriander
- 1 tsp turmeric
- 1 tsp smoked paprika
- 1/2 tsp salt
- 1/2 tsp black pepper
- 1 tbsp olive oil
- 4 burger buns, sliced
- Lettuce leaves
- Sliced tomato
- Sliced red onion and coriander leaves, to serve

Instructions:

1. In a mixing bowl, combine the beef mince, grated onion, minced garlic, ground cumin, ground coriander, turmeric, smoked paprika, salt, and black pepper.

2. Mix well using your hands.

3. Divide the mixture into four equal portions and shape each into a burger patty.

4. Preheat the air fryer at 180°C for 3 minutes.

5. Brush the burger patties with olive oil and arrange them on the crisper plate.

6. Air fry for 6 minutes.

7. Flip the burger patties using silicone-tipped tongs and air fry for an additional 6 minutes or until the internal temperature reaches 71°C.

8. Assemble the burgers by placing a lettuce leaf, a burger patty, sliced tomato, sliced red onion, and coriander leaves on each bun.

9. Serve immediately.

Mexican-style pork carnitas

Serves: 4

Prep time: 10 minutes / Cook time: 20 minutes

Ingredients:

- 500g pork shoulder, cut into 2-inch cubes
- 2 tbsp olive oil
- 1 tsp ground cumin
- 1 tsp smoked paprika
- 1 tsp garlic powder
- 1/2 tsp salt
- 1/2 tsp black pepper
- 1 onion, sliced
- 2 garlic cloves, minced
- 120ml chicken stock
- 8 small corn tortillas
- Sliced avocado, chopped cilantro, crumbled cotija cheese, and lime wedges, to serve

Instructions:

1. In a mixing bowl, combine the pork cubes with olive oil, ground cumin, smoked paprika, garlic powder, salt, and black pepper.

2. Mix well.

3. Preheat the air fryer at 180°C for 3 minutes.

4. Arrange the seasoned pork cubes on the crisper plate and air fry for 10 minutes.

5. Add the sliced onion and minced garlic to the crisper plate and air fry for an additional 10 minutes.

6. Pour in the chicken stock and toss everything together.

7. Air fry for 5 more minutes until the pork is tender and crispy.

8. Warm the corn tortillas in the air fryer for 1-2 minutes.

9. Serve the carnitas with the warmed tortillas, sliced avocado, chopped cilantro, crumbled cotija cheese, and lime wedges.

Greek lamb meatballs

Serves: 4

Prep time: 15 minutes / Cook time: 10 minutes

Ingredients:

- 500g lamb mince
- 1/2 onion, grated
- 2 garlic cloves, minced
- 1 egg, lightly beaten
- 1 tsp dried oregano
- 1 tsp dried mint
- 1/2 tsp salt
- 1/4 tsp black pepper
- 1 tbsp olive oil
- Tzatziki, pita bread, sliced cucumber, and cherry tomatoes, to serve

Instructions:

1. In a mixing bowl, combine the lamb mince, grated onion, minced garlic, egg, dried oregano, dried mint, salt, and black pepper.
2. Mix well using your hands.
3. Divide the mixture into twelve equal portions and shape each into a meatball.
4. Preheat the air fryer at 180°C for 3 minutes.
5. Brush the meatballs with olive oil and arrange them on the crisper plate.
6. Air fry for 8-10 minutes.
7. Serve and enjoy!

Caribbean-style beef brisket

Serves: 4

Prep time: 15 minutes / Cook time: 6 hours

Ingredients:

- 1.2 kg beef brisket
- 2 tsp ground allspice
- 1 tsp ground cinnamon
- 1 tsp ground nutmeg
- 1 tsp dried thyme leaves
- 1 tsp garlic powder
- 1 tsp onion powder
- 2 tbsp brown sugar
- 2 tbsp soy sauce
- 1 tbsp Worcestershire sauce
- 1 lime, juiced
- 2 tbsp vegetable oil
- Sea salt and black pepper, to taste

Instructions:

1. In a small bowl, combine allspice, cinnamon, nutmeg, thyme, garlic powder, onion powder, brown sugar, soy sauce, Worcestershire sauce, lime juice, vegetable oil, salt, and black pepper.
2. Mix well and set aside.
3. Place beef brisket in a large bowl and pour the spice mixture over it.
4. Rub the mixture into the meat, making sure it is fully coated.
5. Wrap the brisket tightly with cling film and refrigerate for at least 4 hours, preferably overnight.
6. Preheat the air fryer to 150°C.
7. Remove the beef brisket from the cling film and place it in the air fryer basket.
8. Cook for 6 hours, turning the brisket every 2 hours.
9. After 6 hours, remove the brisket from the air fryer and let it rest for 10 minutes before slicing it.
10. Serve with your choice of sides and enjoy.

Vietnamese-style pork chops

Serves: 2

Prep time: 10 minutes / Cook time: 16 minutes

Ingredients:

- 2 bone-in pork chops (about 400g)
- 2 cloves garlic, minced
- 1 tbsp honey
- 2 tbsp soy sauce
- 1 tbsp fish sauce
- 1 tbsp vegetable oil
- 1 lime, juiced
- Sea salt and black pepper, to taste
- Chopped cilantro and sliced green onions, for garnish

Instructions:

1. In a small bowl, whisk together garlic, honey, soy sauce, fish sauce, vegetable oil, lime juice, salt, and black pepper.

2. Place pork chops in a shallow dish and pour the marinade over them, making sure they are fully coated.
3. Cover and refrigerate for at least 30 minutes.
4. Preheat the air fryer to 200°C.
5. Remove pork chops from the marinade and place them in the air fryer basket.
6. Cook for 16 minutes, flipping the chops halfway through.
7. Once done, remove the chops from the air fryer and let them rest for a few minutes.
8. Garnish with cilantro and green onions before serving.
9. Enjoy with rice or noodles.

Moroccan-style beef skewers

Serves: 4

Prep time: 20 minutes / Cook time: 12 minutes

Ingredients:

- 500g beef sirloin, cut into 2cm cubes
- 1 tsp ground cumin
- 1 tsp ground coriander
- 1 tsp smoked paprika
- 1 tsp ground cinnamon
- 1/2 tsp ground ginger
- 1/2 tsp ground turmeric
- 2 cloves garlic, minced
- 2 tbsp olive oil
- 1 lemon, juiced
- Sea salt and black pepper, to taste
- Wooden skewers, soaked in water for 30 minutes

Instructions:

1. In a small bowl, whisk together cumin, coriander, paprika, cinnamon, ginger, turmeric, garlic, olive oil, lemon juice, salt, and black pepper.
2. Thread the beef cubes onto the soaked wooden skewers.
3. Preheat the air fryer to 200°C.
4. Place the skewers in the air fryer basket and cook for 12 minutes, turning the skewers halfway through.
5. Once done, remove the skewers from the air fryer and let them rest for a few minutes before serving.

French-style lamb chops with dijon mustard

Serves: 2

Prep time: 5 minutes / Cook time: 10 minutes

Ingredients:

- 4 lamb chops (150g each)
- 2 tbsp Dijon mustard
- 2 tbsp olive oil
- 1 tbsp dried thyme
- Sea salt and black pepper, to taste

Instructions:

1. Season the lamb chops with salt, black pepper, and dried thyme on both sides.
2. Spread Dijon mustard evenly on both sides of the chops.
3. Preheat the air fryer to 200°C.
4. Brush both sides of the chops with olive oil and place them in the air fryer basket.
5. Air fry the lamb chops for 10 minutes, flipping them halfway through cooking.
6. Serve with your favourite sides.

Thai-style pork stir-fry

Serves: 2

Prep time: 10 minutes / Cook time: 10 minutes

Ingredients:

- 350g pork tenderloin, sliced thinly
- 2 tbsp vegetable oil
- 2 garlic cloves, minced
- 1 red chilli, deseeded and sliced thinly
- 1 small onion, sliced thinly
- 1 red pepper, sliced thinly
- 100g green beans, trimmed
- 2 tbsp fish sauce
- 2 tbsp soy sauce
- 1 tbsp brown sugar
- A handful of Thai basil leaves

Instructions:

1. Preheat the air fryer to 180°C.
2. In a small bowl, mix together the fish sauce, soy

sauce, and brown sugar.

3. Heat the vegetable oil in a wok or frying pan over high heat.
4. Add the garlic and chilli, and stir-fry for 30 seconds until fragrant.
5. Add the pork and stir-fry for 3-4 minutes until browned.
6. Add the onion, red pepper, and green beans, and stir-fry for another 2-3 minutes until the vegetables are tender but still crisp.
7. Add the fish sauce mixture to the pan and stir-fry for another minute.
8. Turn off the heat, and stir in the Thai basil leaves.
9. Serve with steamed rice.

Jamaican-style oxtail stew

Serves: 4

Prep time: 20 minutes / Cook time: 2 hours

Ingredients:

- 1 kg oxtail
- 2 tbsp vegetable oil
- 1 large onion, chopped
- 4 garlic cloves, minced
- 1 tsp dried thyme
- 1 tsp ground allspice
- 2 tbsp tomato paste
- 2 tbsp Worcestershire sauce
- 2 tbsp brown sugar
- 1 scotch bonnet pepper, seeded and chopped
- 1 can (400g) chopped tomatoes
- 500ml beef stock
- Sea salt and black pepper, to taste

Instructions:

1. Preheat the air fryer to 180°C.
2. Season the oxtail with salt and black pepper on both sides.
3. Heat the vegetable oil in a large skillet or casserole dish over high heat.
4. Add the oxtail and brown on all sides, about 6-8 minutes.
5. Remove the oxtail from the skillet and set aside.
6. Reduce the heat to medium and add the onion and garlic to the skillet.
7. Stir and cook until the onion is soft and

translucent, about 5 minutes.
8. Add the thyme, allspice, tomato paste, Worcestershire sauce, brown sugar, and scotch bonnet pepper to the skillet.
9. Stir and cook for 2-3 minutes until fragrant.
10. Add the chopped tomatoes, beef stock, and oxtail to the skillet.
11. Stir and bring to a simmer.
12. Transfer the mixture to the air fryer basket and cook for 2 hours, stirring occasionally, until the oxtail is tender and falling off the bone.
13. Remove the scotch bonnet pepper before serving with your favourite sides.

Italian-style meatball sub

Serves: 4

Prep time: 20 minutes / Cook time: 20 minutes

Ingredients:

- For the meatballs:
- 450g ground beef
- 120g breadcrumbs
- 120g grated parmesan cheese
- 60g chopped fresh parsley
- 1 egg
- 1 garlic clove, minced
- 1/2 teaspoon salt
- 1/4 teaspoon black pepper
- For the sub:
- 4 sub rolls
- 1/2 cup marinara sauce
- 1/2 cup shredded mozzarella cheese
- 1 tablespoon olive oil
- 1/4 teaspoon garlic powder
- Salt and black pepper, to taste

Instructions:

1. Preheat the air fryer to 180°C.
2. In a large bowl, combine the ground beef, breadcrumbs, parmesan cheese, parsley, egg, garlic, salt, and pepper. Mix well.
3. Shape the mixture into meatballs about the size of a golf ball.
4. Place the meatballs in the air fryer basket and spray them with cooking oil.
5. Cook the meatballs for 10 minutes, turning them

over halfway through.

6. Meanwhile, slice the sub rolls in half lengthwise.
7. In a small bowl, mix together the olive oil, garlic powder, salt, and black pepper.
8. Brush the inside of each sub roll with the olive oil mixture.
9. Spread 1 tablespoon of marinara sauce on the bottom of each sub roll.
10. When the meatballs are cooked, place 3-4 meatballs on top of the marinara sauce in each sub roll.
11. Spoon the remaining marinara sauce over the meatballs.
12. Sprinkle the shredded mozzarella cheese over the marinara sauce.
13. Place the subs in the air fryer basket and cook for an additional 5-7 minutes, or until the cheese is melted and the bread is toasted.
14. Serve the Italian-style meatball subs hot and enjoy!
15. Note: You can serve the subs with additional marinara sauce on the side for dipping, if desired.

Reuben Beef Rolls with Thousand Island Sauce

Serves: Makes 10 rolls

Prep time: 15 minutes / Cook time: 10 minutes per batch

Ingredients:

- 230 g cooked salt beef, chopped
- 120 ml drained and chopped sauerkraut
- 1 (230 g) package cream cheese, softened
- 120 ml shredded Swiss cheese
- 20 slices prosciutto
- Cooking spray
- Thousand Island Sauce:
- 60 ml chopped dill pickles
- 60 ml tomato ketchup
- 180 ml mayonnaise
- Fresh thyme leaves, for garnish
- 2 tablespoons sugar
- ⅛ teaspoon fine sea salt
- Ground black pepper, to taste

Instructions:

1. Preheat the air fryer to 204°C and spritz with cooking spray.
2. Combine the beef, sauerkraut, cream cheese, and Swiss cheese in a large bowl. Stir to mix well.
3. Unroll a slice of prosciutto on a clean work surface, then top with another slice of prosciutto crosswise. Scoop up 4 tablespoons of the beef mixture in the center.
4. Fold the top slice sides over the filling as the ends of the roll, then roll up the long sides of the bottom prosciutto and make it into a roll shape. Overlap the sides by about 1 inch. Repeat with remaining filling and prosciutto.
5. Arrange the rolls in the preheated air fryer, seam side down, and spritz with cooking spray. 6. Air fry for 10 minutes or until golden and crispy. Flip the rolls halfway through. Work in batches to avoid overcrowding. 7. Meanwhile, combine the Ingredients for the sauce in a small bowl. Stir to mix well. 8. Serve the rolls with the dipping sauce.

French Dip Sandwich

Serves: 2

Prep time: 5 minutes / Cook time: 3-5 minutes per batch

Ingredients:

- 4 slices of bread
- 100g of thinly sliced roast beef
- 2 cloves of minced garlic
- 2 tablespoons of beef stock
- 2 tablespoons of butter
- Salt and pepper, to taste

Instructions:

1. Preheat the air fryer to 180 °C.
2. Spread butter on one side of each slice of bread.
3. Place the roast beef between two slices of bread and press the edges together to make a sandwich.
4. Place the sandwich in the air fryer and cook for 3-5 minutes or until the bread is golden brown and the roast beef is heated through, flipping halfway through.
5. Remove from the air fryer and let it cool for a

few minutes before serving.

6..Serve with the beef stock for dipping.

Air Fried Crispy Venison

Serves: 4

Prep time: 10 minutes / Cook time:20 minutes

Ingredients:

- 2 eggs
- 60 ml milk
- 235 ml whole wheat flour
- ½ teaspoon salt
- ¼ teaspoon ground black pepper
- 450 g venison backstrap/striploin, sliced
- Cooking spray

Instructions:

1. Preheat the air fryer to 182ºC and spritz with cooking spray.
2. Whisk the eggs with milk in a large bowl. Combine the flour with salt and ground black pepper in a shallow dish.
3. Dredge the venison in the flour first, then into the egg mixture. Shake the excess off and roll the venison back over the flour to coat well.
4. Arrange half of the venison in the preheated air fryer and spritz with cooking spray.
5. Air fry for 10 minutes or until the internal temperature of the venison reaches at least 64ºC for medium rare. Flip the venison halfway through. Repeat with remaining venison. 6. Serve immediately.

20 Pork Schnitzels with Sour Cream and Dill Sauce

Serves: 4-6

Prep time: 5 minutes / Cook time:24 minutes

Ingredients:

- 120 ml flour
- 1½ teaspoons salt
- Freshly ground black pepper, to taste
- 2 eggs
- 120 ml milk
- 355 ml toasted breadcrumbs
- 1 teaspoon paprika
- 6 boneless pork chops (about 680 g), fat trimmed, pound to ½-inch thick
- 2 tablespoons olive oil
- 3 tablespoons melted butter
- Lemon wedges, for serving
- Sour Cream and Dill Sauce:
- 235 ml chicken stock
- 1½ tablespoons cornflour
- 80 ml sour cream
- 1½ tablespoons chopped fresh dill
- Salt and ground black pepper, to taste

Instructions:

1. Preheat the air fryer to 204ºC.
2. Combine the flour with salt and black pepper in a large bowl. Stir to mix well. Whisk the egg with milk in a second bowl. Stir the breadcrumbs and paprika in a third bowl.
3. Dredge the pork chops in the flour bowl, then in the egg milk, and then into the breadcrumbs bowl. Press to coat well. Shake the excess off.
4. Arrange one pork chop in the preheated air fryer each time, then brush with olive oil and butter on all sides.
5. Air fry each pork chop for 4 minutes or until golden brown and crispy. Flip the chop halfway through the cooking time.
6. Transfer the cooked pork chop (schnitzel) to a baking pan in the oven and keep warm over low heat while air frying the remaining pork chops.
7. Meanwhile, combine the chicken stock and cornflour in a small saucepan and bring to a boil over medium-high heat. Simmer for 2 more minutes.
8. Turn off the heat, then mix in the sour cream, fresh dill, salt, and black pepper.
9. Remove the schnitzels from the air fryer to a plate and baste with sour cream and dill sauce. Squeeze the lemon wedges over and slice to serve.

Herb-Crusted Lamb Chops

Serves: 2

Prep time: 10 minutes / Cook time:5 minutes

Ingredients:

- 1 large egg
- 2 cloves garlic, minced
- 60 ml finely crushed pork scratchings
- 60 ml pre-grated Parmesan cheese
- 1 tablespoon chopped fresh oregano leaves
- 1 tablespoon chopped fresh rosemary leaves
- 1 teaspoon chopped fresh thyme leaves
- ½ teaspoon ground black pepper
- 4 (1-inch-thick) lamb chops
- For Garnish/Serving (Optional):
- Sprigs of fresh oregano
- Sprigs of fresh rosemary
- Sprigs of fresh thyme
- Lavender flowers
- Lemon slices

Instructions:

1. Spray the air fryer basket with avocado oil. Preheat the air fryer to 204ºC.
2. Beat the egg in a shallow bowl, add the garlic, and stir well to combine. In another shallow bowl, mix together the crushed pork scratchings, Parmesan, herbs, and pepper.
3. One at a time, dip the lamb chops into the egg mixture, shake off the excess egg, and then dredge them in the Parmesan mixture. Use your hands to coat the chops well in the Parmesan mixture and form a nice crust on all sides; if necessary, dip the chops again in both the egg and the Parmesan mixture.
4. Place the lamb chops in the air fryer basket, leaving space between them, and air fry for 5 minutes, or until the internal temperature reaches 64ºC for medium doneness. Allow to rest for 10 minutes before serving.
5. Garnish with sprigs of oregano, rosemary, and thyme, and lavender flowers, if desired. Serve with lemon slices, if desired.
6. Best served fresh. Store leftovers in an airtight container in the fridge for up to 4 days. Serve chilled over a salad, or reheat in a 176ºC air fryer for 3 minutes, or until heated through.

Sichuan Cumin Lamb

Serves: 4

Prep time: 30 minutes / Cook time:10 minutes

Ingredients:

- Lamb:
- 2 tablespoons cumin seeds
- 1 teaspoon Sichuan peppercorns, or ½ teaspoon cayenne pepper
- 450 g lamb (preferably shoulder), cut into ½ by 2-inch pieces
- 2 tablespoons vegetable oil
- 1 tablespoon light soy sauce
- 1 tablespoon minced garlic
- 2 fresh red chiles, chopped
- 1 teaspoon coarse or flaky salt
- ¼ teaspoon sugar
- For Serving:
- 2 spring onions, chopped
- Large handful of chopped fresh coriander

Instructions:

1. For the lamb: In a dry skillet, toast the cumin seeds and Sichuan peppercorns (if using) over medium heat, stirring frequently, until fragrant, 1 to 2 minutes. Remove from the heat and let cool. Use a mortar and pestle to coarsely grind the toasted spices.
2. Use a fork to pierce the lamb pieces to allow the marinade to penetrate better. In a large bowl or resealable plastic bag, combine the toasted spices, vegetable oil, soy sauce, garlic, chiles, salt, and sugar. Add the lamb to the bag. Seal and massage to coat. Marinate at room temperature for 30 minutes.
3. Place the lamb in a single layer in the air fryer basket. Set the air fryer to 176ºC for 10 minutes. Use a meat thermometer to ensure the lamb has reached an internal temperature of 64ºC (medium-rare).
4. Transfer the lamb to a serving bowl. Stir in the spring onionspring onions and coriander and serve.

Thai-style shrimp cakes

Serves: 4

Prep time: 15 minutes / Cook time: 12 minutes

Ingredients:

- 300g raw shrimp, peeled and deveined
- 40g chopped fresh coriander
- 45g chopped spring onions
- 2 cloves garlic, minced
- 1 red chilli, seeded and minced
- 1 tbsp fish sauce
- 1 tbsp red curry paste
- 1 egg
- 60g breadcrumbs
- 1 tbsp vegetable oil

Instructions:

1. In a food processor, pulse the shrimp until finely minced.
2. Add coriander, spring onions, garlic, chilli, fish sauce, red curry paste, and egg.
3. Pulse until everything is well combined.
4. Transfer the mixture to a bowl, and add the breadcrumbs.
5. Mix until well combined.
6. Using wet hands, shape the mixture into small cakes and place them on a plate.
7. Preheat the air fryer to 200°C.
8. Brush the shrimp cakes with oil, and place them in the air fryer basket in a single layer.
9. Select air fry at 200°C for 12 minutes.
10. Flip the cakes halfway through the cooking time using silicone-tipped tongs to ensure even cooking.
11. Once cooked, remove the cakes from the air fryer and serve hot with your favourite dipping sauce. Enjoy!

Indian-style samosas

Serves: 12 samosas

Prep time: 30 minutes / Cook time: 20 minutes

Ingredients:

For the filling:

- 1 tbsp vegetable oil
- 1 onion, finely chopped
- 2 potatoes, peeled and diced
- 120g green peas
- 1 tsp cumin powder
- tsp coriander powder
- 1 tsp garam masala powder
- 1/2 tsp turmeric powder
- 1/4 tsp red chilli powder
- Salt, to taste

For the dough:

- 250g plain flour
- 2 tbsp vegetable oil
- 1/2 tsp salt
- 1/2 cup water

Instructions:

For the filling:

1. Heat the oil in a pan over medium heat.
2. Add the onion and sauté until softened.
3. Add the potatoes and cook until they start to soften.
4. Add the peas, cumin powder, coriander powder, garam masala powder, turmeric powder, red chilli powder, and salt.
5. Stir until well combined.
6. Remove from heat and let it cool.

For the dough:

1. In a bowl, mix together the flour and salt.
2. Add the oil and mix until it resembles breadcrumbs.
3. Gradually add the water and knead until it forms a smooth dough.
4. Cover and set aside for 15 minutes.
5. Divide the dough into 6 equal portions.
6. Roll each portion into a ball and flatten it slightly.
7. Roll each portion into a circle about 6 inches in diameter.
8. Cut each circle in half to form two semi-circles.
9. Brush the edges of each semicircle with water.
10. Form a cone by bringing the two edges of the semi-circle together, and seal the edges together by pressing firmly.
11. Fill the cones with the prepared filling and seal the top by pressing the edges together.
12. Preheat the air fryer to 180°C.

13. Brush the samosas with oil, and place them in the air fryer basket in a single layer.
14. Select air fry at 180°C for 20 minutes.
15. Once cooked, remove the samosas from the air fryer and serve hot with your favourite chutney. Enjoy!

Italian-style arancini balls

Serves: 4

Prep time: 20 minutes / Cook time: 16 minutes

Ingredients:

- 250g Arborio rice
- 500ml vegetable stock
- 1 onion, chopped
- 2 garlic cloves, minced
- 1 tbsp olive oil
- 100g grated Parmesan cheese
- 150g mozzarella cheese, diced
- 50g plain flour
- 1 large egg, beaten
- 100g panko breadcrumbs
- 1 tsp dried oregano
- Salt and pepper, to taste
- 2 tsp olive oil

Instructions:

1. In a large pot, heat the olive oil over medium heat. Add the chopped onions and garlic and sauté until softened, about 5 minutes.
2. Add the Arborio rice and stir to coat with the onion and garlic mixture. Cook for 1-2 minutes until the rice starts to toast.
3. Pour in the vegetable stock, one ladle at a time, stirring constantly and adding more as the liquid is absorbed. Cook until the rice is tender but still has a slight bite.
4. Remove the pot from heat and stir in the grated Parmesan cheese and diced mozzarella cheese. Season with salt and pepper to taste. Allow the mixture to cool for 10 minutes.
5. Scoop the rice mixture into balls, approximately 2 tablespoons each, and roll them into smooth, compact balls. Place the balls on a plate and chill for 30 minutes.
6. Preheat the air fryer to 200°C.
7. Place the plain flour in one shallow dish, the beaten egg in another, and the panko breadcrumbs mixed with dried oregano in another dish.
8. Roll the chilled arancini balls in the flour, then dip in the egg, and finally coat in the panko breadcrumb mixture.
9. Arrange the prepared arancini balls in the air fryer basket and spray with 1 teaspoon of olive oil.
10. Select air fry 200°C for 8 minutes
11. When the time reaches 4 minutes, turn the arancini balls over using silicone-tipped tongs and spray with cooking oil on the other side. Reinsert the drawer to continue cooking.
12. Serve the arancini balls warm, garnished with fresh basil leaves and a side of marinara sauce for dipping.

Chinese-style pork dumplings

Serves: 4-6

Prep time: 45 minutes / Cook time: 10 minutes

Ingredients:

- For the dumpling filling:
- 250g ground pork
- 1 tbsp soy sauce
- 1 tbsp sesame oil
- 2 tbsp finely chopped scallions
- 2 cloves garlic, minced
- 1 tbsp cornstarch
- 1/4 tsp ground black pepper
- 60g water chestnuts, finely chopped
- 60g bamboo shoots, finely chopped
- For the dumpling wrappers:
- 200g all-purpose flour
- 120ml boiling water
- Extra flour for dusting
- For the dipping sauce:
- 2 tbsp soy sauce
- 1 tbsp rice vinegar
- 1 tsp sesame oil
- 1 tbsp finely chopped scallions

Instructions:

1. In a mixing bowl, combine all the filling Ingredients and mix well until fully combined. Set aside.
2. In another mixing bowl, add the flour and make a well in the centre. Slowly pour the boiling water while mixing the flour with chopsticks or a fork until the dough forms. Knead the dough for 5 minutes until it becomes smooth and elastic.
3. Dust your working surface with flour and roll out the dough into a thin log. Cut the log into 24 equal pieces. Roll each piece into a ball and

flatten it into a small disc with a rolling pin.

4. Place a spoonful of filling into the centre of the disc. Fold the wrapper in half and pleat the edges to seal the dumpling. Repeat until all the filling and wrappers are used.
5. Preheat the air fryer to 200°C for 5 minutes. Arrange the dumplings on the crisper plate, making sure they do not touch.
6. Spray the dumplings with cooking oil and air fry for 10 minutes until the wrappers are golden and crispy.
7. In a small bowl, mix all the dipping sauce Ingredients together.
8. Serve the dumplings hot with the dipping sauce on the side.

Mexican-style churros

Serves: 4-6

Prep time: 10 minutes / Cook time: 10 minutes

Ingredients:

- 1 cup water
- 120g unsalted butter
- 1/4 tsp salt
- 240g all-purpose flour
- 3 eggs
- 1 tsp vanilla extract
- 60g granulated sugar
- 1 tsp ground cinnamon

Instructions:

1. In a medium saucepan, bring the water, butter, and salt to a boil. Reduce heat to low and add the flour, stirring constantly with a wooden spoon until the dough forms a ball and pulls away from the sides of the pan.
2. Remove from heat and let cool for 2-3 minutes. Add the eggs one at a time, beating well after each addition, until the dough becomes smooth and glossy. Add the vanilla extract and mix well.
3. Preheat the air fryer to 180°C for 5 minutes.
4. Transfer the churro dough into a piping bag with a star-shaped nozzle. Pipe long churros onto the crisper plate, leaving enough space between them.
5. Air fry the churros for 10 minutes, or until they are golden brown and crispy.

6. In a shallow dish, mix the sugar and cinnamon together.
7. When the churros are done, remove them from the air fryer and roll them in the cinnamon-sugar mixture until they are coated evenly.
8. Serve the churros warm.

Greek-style spanakopita

Serves: 4

Prep time: 30 minutes / Cook time: 20 minutes

Ingredients:

- 250g fresh spinach, washed and chopped
- 150g feta cheese, crumbled
- 1 onion, chopped
- 2 garlic cloves, minced
- 2 eggs
- 2 tbsp olive oil
- 1 tsp dried dill
- 1 tsp dried mint
- 1/4 tsp grated nutmeg
- Salt and black pepper, to taste
- 8 sheets filo pastry
- 60g butter, melted

Instructions:

1. Preheat the air fryer to 180°C.
2. In a pan over medium heat, add 1 tablespoon of olive oil and sauté the onion until translucent.
3. Add the minced garlic and sauté for another minute.
4. Add the chopped spinach and cook until wilted.
5. Remove from heat and let it cool down.
6. In a bowl, beat the eggs and add crumbled feta cheese, dill, mint, nutmeg, salt, and pepper.
7. Mix well.
8. Add the spinach mixture and stir until well combined.
9. Brush each sheet of filo pastry with melted butter and place them on top of each other.
10. Cut the stacked filo pastry sheets in half lengthwise to make two long strips.
11. Spoon the spinach mixture along the bottom edge of the filo pastry strip, leaving a 1cm border at the bottom and sides.
12. Fold the sides of the pastry over the filling and roll up the pastry tightly from the bottom to the top.
13. Brush the spanakopita with butter and place them in the air fryer basket.
14. Cook for 20 minutes or until golden brown and

crispy. Serve hot or at room temperature.

15. Enjoy your delicious Greek-style Spanakopita!

Japanese-style takoyaki

Serves: 4

Prep time: 20 minutes / Cook time: 10 minutes

Ingredients:

- 150g all-purpose flour
- 1/2 tsp baking powder
- 1/2 tsp salt
- 2 eggs
- 500ml dashi stock
- 120g chopped octopus
- 4 spring onions, finely chopped
- 1 tbsp soy sauce
- 1 tbsp vegetable oil
- Takoyaki sauce, to serve
- Mayonnaise, to serve
- Aonori (dried green seaweed flakes), to serve
- Katsuobushi (dried bonito flakes), to serve

Instructions:

1. In a large bowl, sift together the flour, baking powder, and salt.
2. In a separate bowl, beat the eggs and dashi stock together.
3. Add the egg mixture to the flour mixture and whisk until smooth.
4. Stir in the chopped octopus, spring onions, and soy sauce.
5. Preheat the air fryer to 180°C.
6. Brush the takoyaki mould with vegetable oil.
7. Pour the batter into the takoyaki mould, filling each hole to the top.
8. Cook the takoyaki for 5 minutes, then use a skewer or chopstick to turn each ball a quarter-turn.
9. Continue cooking the takoyaki for another 5 minutes, turning each ball a quarter-turn every minute or so, until they are golden brown and crispy on the outside.
10. Serve the takoyaki hot with takoyaki sauce, mayonnaise, aonori, and katsuobushi.

Jamaican-style plantain chips

Serves: 4

Prep time: 10 minutes / Cook time: 10 minutes

Ingredients:

- 2 large green plantains
- 2 tbsp vegetable oil
- 1/2 tsp salt
- 1/4 tsp ground black pepper
- 1/4 tsp cayenne pepper (optional)

Instructions:

1. Peel the plantains and slice them into thin rounds.
2. In a large bowl, toss the plantain slices with the vegetable oil, salt, black pepper, and cayenne pepper (if using).
3. Preheat the air fryer to 200°C.
4. Spread the plantain slices in a single layer in the air fryer basket.
5. Cook the plantain slices for 5 minutes, then shake the basket to flip the slices.
6. Continue cooking the plantain slices for another 5 minutes, or until they are golden brown and crispy.
7. Serve the plantain chips hot as a snack or side dish.

Spanish-style croquetas

Serves: 2

Prep time: 30 minutes / Cook time: 12 minutes

Ingredients:

- 50g butter
- 1/2 onion, finely chopped
- 100g plain flour
- 400ml milk
- 1/2 tsp salt
- 1/4 tsp ground nutmeg
- 150g cooked ham, finely chopped
- 50g grated Manchego cheese
- 2 eggs
- 100g breadcrumbs

Instructions:

1. Melt the butter in a saucepan over medium heat.
2. Add the onion and sauté for 5-7 minutes, until it is softened but not browned.
3. Add the flour to the pan and stir until it forms a smooth paste.
4. Cook for 2-3 minutes, stirring constantly.
5. Gradually add the milk, whisking constantly to prevent lumps from forming.
6. Cook for 10-12 minutes, until the mixture has thickened and coats the back of a spoon.
7. Stir in the salt and nutmeg.

8. Add the ham and Manchego cheese to the pan and stir until the cheese is melted and the ham is evenly distributed.
9. Allow the mixture to cool for 10-15 minutes.
10. Using wet hands, shape the cooled mixture into small, oval-shaped croquetas.
11. In a shallow dish, beat the eggs.
12. In a separate shallow dish, place the breadcrumbs.
13. Dip each croqueta into the beaten egg, then roll it in the breadcrumbs to coat evenly.
14. Arrange the croquetas in a single layer on the crisper plate.
15. Air fry at 200°C for 12 minutes.
16. When the cooking time is up, remove the croquetas from the air fryer and transfer them to a serving dish. Serve immediately.

Cajun-style popcorn shrimp

Serves: 4

Prep time: 10 minutes / Cook time: 10 minutes

Ingredients:

- 300g raw shrimp, peeled and deveined
- 80g all-purpose flour
- 2 tsp Cajun seasoning
- 1 tsp garlic powder
- 1/2 tsp smoked paprika
- 1/4 tsp cayenne pepper (optional)
- 1 large egg, beaten
- 50g breadcrumbs
- Cooking spray

Instructions:

1. In a shallow dish, combine the flour, Cajun seasoning, garlic powder, smoked paprika, and cayenne pepper (if using).
2. In another shallow dish, beat the egg.
3. In a third shallow dish, add the breadcrumbs.
4. Dip each shrimp into the flour mixture, then the egg, and finally the breadcrumbs, pressing the breadcrumbs into the shrimp to ensure they are coated well.
5. Place the breaded shrimp in a single layer in the air fryer basket.
6. Spray the shrimp with cooking spray.
7. Select air fry at 200°C for 10 minutes.
8. Halfway through cooking, shake the air fryer basket to ensure the shrimp cook evenly.
9. Serve with your favourite dipping sauce and enjoy!

Italian-style pizza rolls

Serves: 4

Prep time: 10 minutes / Cook time: 8 minutes

Ingredients:

- 1 can refrigerated pizza dough (260g)
- 80g pepperoni slices, chopped
- 60g grated mozzarella cheese
- 50g pizza sauce
- 1/4 tsp garlic powder
- 1/4 tsp dried basil
- 1/4 tsp dried oregano
- 1/4 tsp salt
- Cooking spray

Instructions:

1. Preheat the air fryer to 200°C.
2. Unroll the pizza dough onto a lightly floured surface.
3. Spread the pizza sauce over the dough, leaving a 1/2-inch border around the edges.
4. Sprinkle the pepperoni and mozzarella cheese on top of the pizza sauce.
5. Sprinkle the garlic powder, dried basil, dried oregano, and salt on top of the pepperoni and cheese.
6. Roll the pizza dough up tightly and cut into 8 equal slices.
7. Place the pizza rolls in the air fryer basket, making sure they are not touching.
8. Spray the pizza rolls with cooking spray.
9. Select air fry at 200°C for 8 minutes.
10. Serve hot and enjoy!

Lebanese-style kibbeh balls

Serves: 4

Prep time: 20 minutes / Cook time: 12 minutes

Ingredients:

- 200g ground beef
- 100g bulgur wheat, soaked in water for 15 minutes and drained

- 1 small onion, finely chopped
- 1/4 tsp cinnamon   · 1/4 tsp allspice
- 1/4 tsp ground cumin · 1/4 tsp salt
- 1/4 tsp black pepper · Cooking spray

Instructions:

1. Preheat the air fryer to 200°C.
2. In a mixing bowl, combine the ground beef, soaked bulgur wheat, onion, cinnamon, allspice, cumin, salt, and black pepper. Mix well.
3. Shape the mixture into small balls, approximately the size of a golf ball.
4. Place the kibbeh balls in the air fryer basket, making sure they are not touching.
5. Spray the kibbeh balls with cooking spray.
6. Select air fry at 200°C for 12 minutes.
7. Halfway through cooking, shake the air fryer basket to ensure the kibbeh balls cook evenly.
8. Serve hot and enjoy!

Moroccan-style vegetable pastries

Serves: 4

Prep time: 30 minutes / Cook time: 15 minutes

Ingredients:

For the pastry:

- 250g plain flour   · 1/2 tsp salt
- 1/2 tsp ground turmeric
- 1/2 tsp ground cumin · 1/2 tsp paprika
- 1/2 tsp ground coriander
- 120g unsalted butter, chilled and diced
- 4-5 tbsp cold water

For the filling:

- 1 small onion, finely chopped
- 2 garlic cloves, minced
- 1 tsp ground cumin   · 1 tsp ground coriander
- 1/2 tsp paprika   · 1/2 tsp ground cinnamon
- 1/2 tsp ground ginger · 1/4 tsp ground nutmeg
- 1/4 tsp cayenne pepper
- 400g canned chickpeas, drained and rinsed
- 200g canned chopped tomatoes
- 1 medium sweet potato, peeled and diced
- 1 medium courgette, diced
- 2 tbsp chopped fresh coriander leaves
- 1 tbsp lemon juice
- Salt and black pepper, to taste

Instructions:

1. To make the pastry, combine the flour, salt, and spices in a large mixing bowl. Add the diced butter and use your fingertips to rub the butter into the flour mixture until the mixture resembles breadcrumbs.
2. Gradually add cold water, a tablespoon at a time, until the mixture comes together to form a dough. Knead the dough for a few minutes until smooth, then cover it with cling film and chill for 30 minutes.
3. To make the filling, heat a tablespoon of oil in a frying pan over medium heat.
4. Add the chopped onion and garlic and cook for a few minutes until softened. Add the spices and cook for another minute until fragrant.
5. Add the
6. chickpeas, tomatoes, sweet potato, and courgette to the pan and stir to combine. Cook for 10-12 minutes until the vegetables are tender.
7. Stir in the fresh coriander and lemon juice, and season with salt and black pepper to taste.
8. Preheat the air fryer to 180°C.
9. Divide the pastry dough into 8 equal pieces and roll each piece out into a circle about 12 cm in diameter.
10. Spoon a heaped tablespoon of the vegetable filling onto one half of each circle, leaving a 1cm border around the edge.
11. Fold the pastry over to enclose the filling and crimp the edges to seal.
12. Place the pastries in the air fryer basket and cook for 15 minutes until golden and crisp.
13. Serve hot or cold.

Filipino-style lumpia

Serves: 4

Prep time: 30 minutes / Cook time: 10 minutes

Ingredients:

For the filling:

- 250g minced pork
- 1 large carrot, peeled and grated
- 1 large onion, chopped
- 2 garlic cloves, minced
- 50g green beans, chopped

- 50g bean sprouts
- 1 tbsp oyster sauce
- Salt and black pepper, to taste
- 12-16 spring roll wrappers
- 1 tbsp soy sauce
- 1 tbsp cornflour

For the dipping sauce:
- 2 tbsp soy sauce
- 1 tbsp brown sugar
- 1 red chilli, finely chopped
- 1 tbsp rice vinegar
- 1 garlic clove, minced

Instructions:

1. To make the filling, heat a tablespoon of oil in a frying pan over medium heat.
2. Add the chopped onion and garlic and cook for a few minutes until softened.
3. Add the minced pork and cook for 5-6 minutes until browned.
4. Add the grated carrot, green beans, and bean sprouts to the pan and stir to combine.
5. Cook for another 2-3 minutes until the vegetables are tender.
6. Stir in the soy sauce, oyster sauce, and cornflour.
7. Preheat the air fryer to 190°C.
8. To assemble the lumpia, take a spring roll wrapper and place it in a diamond shape on a clean surface. Spoon some of the pork and vegetable filling onto the wrapper, leaving a 2cm border at the bottom. Fold the bottom edge up and over the filling, then fold in the sides. Roll the wrapper tightly upwards, forming a cigar shape. Dab a little bit of water on the top edge to seal the roll.
9. Place the lumpia rolls in the air fryer basket, leaving a little bit of space between each one.
10. Spray the rolls with cooking spray.
11. Cook for 8-10 minutes, flipping them over halfway through the cooking time, until they are golden brown and crispy.
12. Serve hot with sweet chilli sauce or your favourite dipping sauce. Enjoy!

Air Fryer Ranch Seasoned Pretzel Bites

Serves: 6-8

Prep time: 10 minutes / Cook time: 10 minutes

Ingredients:

- 450g pretzel bites
- 60g butter, melted
- 2 tablespoons ranch seasoning mix
- 1/4 teaspoon garlic powder
- 1/4 teaspoon onion powder
- 1/4 teaspoon dried dill

Instructions:

1. Preheat the air fryer to 180°C.
2. In a small bowl, combine the melted butter, ranch seasoning mix, garlic powder, onion powder, and dried dill.
3. Place the pretzel bites in the air fryer basket, and pour the butter mixture over the top. Toss to coat evenly.
4. Cook the pretzel bites in the air fryer for 8-10 minutes, or until they are golden brown and crispy.
5. Remove the pretzel bites from the air fryer, and let them cool for a few minutes before serving.

Shishito Peppers with Herb Dressing

Serves: 2-4

Prep time: 10 minutes / Cook time: 6 minutes

Ingredients:

- 170 g Shishito peppers
- 1 tablespoon vegetable oil
- Kosher or coarse sea salt and freshly ground black pepper, to taste
- 125 g mayonnaise
- 2 tablespoons finely chopped fresh basil leaves
- 2 tablespoons finely chopped fresh flat-leaf parsley
- 1 tablespoon finely chopped fresh tarragon
- 1 tablespoon finely chopped fresh chives
- Finely grated zest of ½ lemon
- 1 tablespoon fresh lemon juice
- Flaky sea salt, for serving

Instructions:

1. Preheat the air fryer to 204ºC.
2. In a bowl, toss together the Shishitos and oil to evenly coat and season with kosher salt and black pepper. Transfer to the air fryer and air

fry for 6 minutes, shaking the basket halfway through, or until the Shishitos are blistered and lightly charred.

3. Meanwhile, in a small bowl, whisk together the mayonnaise, basil, parsley, tarragon, chives, lemon zest, and lemon juice.

4. Pile the peppers on a plate, sprinkle with flaky sea salt, and serve hot with the dressing.

Lemony Pear Chips

Serves: 4

Prep time: 15 minutes / Cook time: 9-13 minutes

Ingredients:

- 2 firm Bosc pears, cut crosswise into ⅛-inch-thick slices
- 1 tablespoon freshly squeezed lemon juice
- ½ teaspoon ground cinnamon
- ⅛ teaspoon ground cardamom

Instructions:

1. Preheat the air fryer to 192°C.
2. Separate the smaller stem-end pear rounds from the larger rounds with seeds. Remove the core and seeds from the larger slices. Sprinkle all slices with lemon juice, cinnamon, and cardamom.
3. Put the smaller chips into the air fryer basket. Air fry for 3 to 5 minutes, or until light golden brown, shaking the basket once during cooking. Remove from the air fryer.
4. Repeat with the larger slices, air frying for 6 to 8 minutes, or until light golden brown, shaking the basket once during cooking.
5. Remove the chips from the air fryer. Cool and serve or store in an airtight container at room temperature up for to 2 days.

Air Fryer Hashbrowns Recipe

Serves: 4

Prep time: 10 minutes / Cook time: 10-15 minutes

Ingredients:

- 500 g grated potatoes

- 2 tbsp olive oil
- 1 tsp onion powder
- Salt and pepper, to taste
- 50 g shredded cheddar cheese (optional)

Instructions:

1. Preheat the air fryer to 400°F (200°C).
2. In a large bowl, mix together the grated potatoes, olive oil, onion powder, salt, and pepper.
3. Place spoonfuls of the potato mixture into the air fryer basket, pressing down slightly to form compact patties.
4. Cook the hash browns for 10-15 minutes, or until they are crispy and golden brown, flipping them once during cooking.
5. If desired, sprinkle the shredded cheddar cheese over the hash browns during the last 2-3 minutes of cooking, until the cheese is melted.
6. Serve the hash browns immediately, topped with chopped fresh parsley or chives, if desired.

20 Crispy Mozzarella Sticks

Serves: 4

Prep time: 8 minutes / Cook time: 5 minutes

Ingredients:

- 120 ml plain flour
- 1 egg, beaten
- 120 ml panko breadcrumbs
- 120 ml grated Parmesan cheese
- 1 teaspoon Italian seasoning
- ½ teaspoon garlic salt
- 6 Mozzarella sticks, halved crosswise
- Olive oil spray

Instructions:

1. Put the flour in a small bowl.
2. Put the beaten egg in another small bowl.
3. In a medium bowl, stir together the panko, Parmesan cheese, Italian seasoning, and garlic salt.
4. Roll a Mozzarella-stick half in the flour, dip it into the egg, and then roll it in the panko mixture to coat. Press the coating lightly to make sure the breadcrumbs stick to the cheese. Repeat with the remaining 11 Mozzarella sticks.
5. Insert the crisper plate into the basket and the

basket into the unit. Preheat the unit by selecting AIR FRY, setting the temperature to 204ºC, and setting the time to 3 minutes. Select START/ STOP to begin. 6. Once the unit is preheated, spray the crisper plate with olive oil and place a parchment paper liner in the basket. Place the Mozzarella sticks into the basket and lightly spray them with olive oil. 7. Select AIR FRY, set the temperature to 204ºC, and set the time to 5 minutes. Select START/STOP to begin. 8. When the cooking is complete, the Mozzarella sticks should be golden and crispy. Let the sticks stand for 1 minute before transferring them to a serving plate. Serve warm.

Chilli-Brined Fried Calamari

Serves: 2

Prep time: 20 minutes / Cook time: 8 minutes

Ingredients:

- 1 (227 g) jar sweet or hot pickled cherry peppers
- 227 g calamari bodies and tentacles, bodies cut into ½-inch-wide rings
- 1 lemon
- 475 ml plain flour
- Rock salt and freshly ground black pepper, to taste
- 3 large eggs, lightly beaten
- Cooking spray
- 120 ml mayonnaise
- 1 teaspoon finely chopped rosemary
- 1 garlic clove, minced

Instructions:

1. Drain the pickled pepper brine into a large bowl and tear the peppers into bite-size strips. Add the pepper strips and calamari to the brine and let stand in the refrigerator for 20 minutes or up to 2 hours.
2. Grate the lemon zest into a large bowl then whisk

in the flour and season with salt and pepper. Dip the calamari and pepper strips in the egg, then toss them in the flour mixture until fully coated. Spray the calamari and peppers liberally with cooking spray, then transfer half to the air fryer. Air fry at 204ºC, shaking the basket halfway into cooking, until the calamari is cooked through and golden brown, about 8 minutes. Transfer to a plate and repeat with the remaining pieces.

3. In a small bowl, whisk together the mayonnaise, rosemary, and garlic. Squeeze half the zested lemon to get 1 tablespoon of juice and stir it into the sauce. Season with salt and pepper. Cut the remaining zested lemon half into 4 small wedges and serve alongside the calamari, peppers, and sauce.

Crispy Breaded Beef Cubes

Serves: 4

Prep time: 10 minutes / Cook time: 12-16 minutes

Ingredients:

- 450 g sirloin tip, cut into 1-inch cubes
- 240 ml cheese pasta sauce
- 355 ml soft breadcrumbs
- 2 tablespoons olive oil
- ½ teaspoon dried marjoram

Instructions:

1. Preheat the air fryer to 182ºC.
2. In a medium bowl, toss the beef with the pasta sauce to coat.
3. In a shallow bowl, combine the breadcrumbs, oil, and marjoram, and mix well. Drop the beef cubes, one at a time, into the bread crumb mixture to coat thoroughly.
4. Air fry the beef in two batches for 6 to 8 minutes, shaking the basket once during cooking time, until the beef is at least 63ºC and the outside is crisp and brown.
5. Serve hot.

Crispy zucchini fries

Serves: 2-4

Prep time: 15 minutes / Cook time: 15 minutes

Ingredients:

- 2 medium zucchinis, sliced into thin fries
- 60g plain flour
- 1 tsp garlic powder
- 1 tsp onion powder
- 1 tsp paprika
- 1/2 tsp salt
- 1/4 tsp black pepper
- 1 large egg, beaten
- 50g panko breadcrumbs
- Cooking spray

Instructions:

1. Preheat the air fryer to 200°C for 5 minutes.
2. In a shallow bowl, mix together the flour, garlic powder, onion powder, paprika, salt, and black pepper.
3. In another shallow bowl, beat the egg.
4. In a third shallow bowl, add the panko breadcrumbs.
5. Dip each zucchini fry in the flour mixture, shaking off any excess. Then dip it into the beaten egg, and finally coat it in the panko breadcrumbs.
6. Spray the air fryer basket with cooking spray, and place the coated zucchini fries in a single layer.
7. Air fry for 10-12 minutes or until golden and crispy, flipping halfway through. Serve hot.

Indian-style vegetable pakoras

Serves: 4

Prep time: 15 minutes / Cook time: 10 minutes

Ingredients:

- 120g chickpea flour
- 1/2 tsp baking powder
- 1/2 tsp ground cumin
- 1/2 tsp ground coriander
- 1/2 tsp garam masala
- 1/2 tsp salt
- 1/4 tsp cayenne pepper
- 120ml water
- 1 medium onion, sliced
- 1 medium potato, peeled and sliced into thin rounds
- 1 medium carrot, peeled and sliced into thin rounds
- 60g chopped spinach
- Cooking spray

Instructions:

1. Preheat the air fryer to 200°C for 5 minutes.
2. In a large mixing bowl, whisk together the chickpea flour, baking powder, cumin, coriander, garam masala, salt, and cayenne pepper.
3. Gradually whisk in the water to form a smooth batter.
4. Add the sliced onion, potato, carrot, and spinach to the batter and mix well.
5. Spray the air fryer basket with cooking spray and spoon the vegetable mixture into the basket in small portions.
6. Air fry for 8-10 minutes, flipping halfway through, or until the pakoras are golden brown and cooked through.
7. Serve hot with chutney or ketchup.

Spicy cauliflower bites

Serves: 2-4

Prep time: 15 minutes / Cook time: 15 minutes

Ingredients:

- 1 small head cauliflower, cut into bite-sized florets
- 60g plain flour
- 1/2 tsp garlic powder
- 1/2 tsp onion powder
- 1 tsp paprika
- 1/2 tsp salt
- 1/4 tsp black pepper
- 120ml milk
- 1 large egg, beaten

- 50g panko breadcrumbs
- 1 tsp hot sauce
- Cooking spray

Instructions:

1. Preheat the air fryer to 200°C for 5 minutes.
2. In a shallow bowl, mix together the flour, garlic powder, onion powder, paprika, salt, and black pepper.
3. In another shallow bowl, whisk together the milk, beaten egg, and hot sauce.
4. In a third shallow bowl, place the panko breadcrumbs.
5. Dip each cauliflower floret into the flour mixture, then into the milk mixture, and finally into the breadcrumbs, pressing gently to adhere.
6. Spray the air fryer basket with cooking spray and arrange the coated cauliflower florets in a single layer. Select air fry at 200°C for 10-12 minutes, flipping the florets halfway through cooking until they are golden brown and crispy on all sides.
7. Serve hot with your favourite dipping sauce, such as spicy mayo or ranch dressing. Enjoy!

Korean-style tofu bowls

Serves: 2-4

Prep time: 20 minutes / Cook time: 20 minutes

Ingredients:

- For the Tofu:
- 400g firm tofu, pressed and cut into cubes
- 2 tbsp cornstarch
- 1/2 tsp garlic powder
- 1/2 tsp onion powder
- 1/2 tsp salt
- 1/4 tsp black pepper
- 2 tbsp gochujang (Korean chilli paste)
- 1 tbsp soy sauce
- 1 tbsp honey
- 1 tbsp rice vinegar
- 1 tbsp sesame oil
- For the Bowls:
- 500g cooked brown rice
- 400g mixed vegetables (carrots, bell peppers, cabbage, mushrooms, etc.)
- 1 tbsp vegetable oil
- 1 tbsp soy sauce

- 1 tbsp sesame oil
- Sesame seeds, for garnish
- Green onions, chopped, for garnish

Instructions:

1. Preheat the air fryer to 200°C for 5 minutes.
2. In a large bowl, combine the cornstarch, garlic powder, onion powder, salt, and black pepper.
3. Add the tofu cubes and toss to coat.
4. In another bowl, whisk together the gochujang, soy sauce, honey, rice vinegar, and sesame oil.
5. Set aside. Place the tofu cubes in the air fryer basket, and cook for 15 minutes, shaking the basket every 5 minutes for even cooking.
6. While the tofu is cooking, heat the vegetable oil in a pan over medium-high heat.
7. Add the mixed vegetables and stir-fry for 3-5 minutes, until tender.
8. Add the soy sauce and sesame oil to the vegetables, and stir to combine.
9. Divide the cooked rice among the bowls. Top with the cooked vegetables and tofu.
10. Drizzle the gochujang sauce over the top, and garnish with sesame seeds and chopped green onions.

Greek-style stuffed peppers

Serves: 4

Prep time: 15 minutes / Cook time: 25 minutes

Ingredients:

- 4 bell peppers, halved and seeded
- 300g lean ground beef
- 1/2 onion, finely chopped
- 1 garlic clove, minced
- 1 tsp dried oregano
- 1 tsp dried basil
- 1/2 tsp salt
- 1/4 tsp black pepper
- 120g cup cooked rice
- 60g crumbled feta cheese
- 1 tbsp olive oil

Instructions:

1. Preheat the air fryer to 200°C for 5 minutes.
2. In a large bowl, combine the ground beef, onion,

garlic, oregano, basil, salt, black pepper, cooked rice, and crumbled feta cheese.

3. Mix well.
4. Stuff each pepper half with the beef mixture.
5. Brush the peppers with olive oil.
6. Place the stuffed peppers in the air fryer basket, and cook for 25 minutes, or until the peppers are tender and the beef is cooked through.
7. Serve and enjoy!

Middle Eastern-style falafel burgers

Serves: 4

Prep time: 20 minutes / Cook time: 20 minutes

Ingredients:

- 1 can chickpeas, drained and rinsed
- 1/2 onion, finely chopped
- 2 garlic cloves, minced
- 2 tbsp chopped fresh parsley
- 1 tbsp chopped fresh cilantro
- 1 tsp ground cumin
- 1 tsp ground coriander
- 1/2 tsp salt
- 1/4 tsp black pepper
- 2 tbsp all-purpose flour
- 1 tbsp olive oil
- 4 burger buns
- Lettuce, sliced tomatoes, sliced red onions, and tzatziki sauce, for serving

Instructions:

1. Preheat the air fryer to 200°C for 5 minutes.
2. In a food processor, pulse the chickpeas, onion, garlic, parsley, cilantro, cumin, coriander, salt, and black pepper until coarsely chopped.
3. Add the flour and pulse until the mixture is well combined and holds together when squeezed.
4. Divide the mixture into 4 equal portions and shape them into patties.
5. Brush each patty with olive oil on both sides.
6. Arrange the patties on the crisper plate of the air fryer and spray them with cooking spray.
7. Select air fry at 200°C for 10 minutes.
8. When the time reaches 5 minutes, flip the patties

over using silicone-tipped tongs and spray them with cooking spray on the other side.

9. Reinsert the drawer to continue cooking.
10. Assemble the burgers on the buns with lettuce, sliced tomatoes, sliced red onions, and tzatziki sauce.
11. Serve immediately and enjoy!

Italian-style eggplant parmesan

Serves: 4

Prep time: 20 minutes / Cook time: 20 minutes

Ingredients:

- 1 large eggplant, sliced into
- 1/4-inch rounds
- 130g all-purpose flour
- 2 large eggs, beaten
- 240g panko breadcrumbs
- 120g grated Parmesan cheese
- 1 tsp dried oregano
- 1 tsp dried basil
- 1/2 tsp garlic powder
- 1/4 tsp salt
- 1/4 tsp black pepper
- 60ml olive oil
- 200ml marinara sauce
- 220g shredded mozzarella cheese
- Fresh basil leaves, for garnish

Instructions:

1. Preheat the air fryer to 200°C for 5 minutes.
2. In a shallow dish, add the flour.
3. In another shallow dish, beat the eggs.
4. In a third shallow dish, mix together the panko breadcrumbs,
5. Parmesan cheese, oregano, basil, garlic powder, salt, and pepper.
6. Coat each eggplant round in flour, then dip into the beaten eggs, and finally coat in the breadcrumb mixture.
7. Place the breaded eggplant rounds on the crisper plate and brush them with olive oil.
8. Select air fry at 200°C for 10 minutes.
9. Flip the eggplant rounds over and brush with more olive oil.
10. Air fry for another 10 minutes.

11. Remove the eggplant rounds from the air fryer and place them in a baking dish.
12. Spoon marinara sauce over each round and sprinkle shredded mozzarella cheese on top.
13. Bake in the oven at 180°C for 10-15 minutes or until the cheese is melted and bubbly.
14. Garnish with fresh basil leaves and serve hot.

Jamaican-style jerk tofu

Serves: 4

Prep time: 20 minutes / Cook time: 20 minutes

Ingredients:

- 1 block (400g) firm tofu, pressed and sliced into 1/2-inch thick pieces
- 60g Jamaican jerk seasoning
- 2 tbsp olive oil 1 lime, juiced
- Salt and pepper, to taste
- Fresh cilantro leaves, for garnish

Instructions:

1. Preheat the air fryer to 200°C for 5 minutes.
2. In a shallow dish, add the Jamaican jerk seasoning.
3. Coat each tofu slice in the seasoning mixture.
4. Place the seasoned tofu slices on the crisper plate and brush them with olive oil.
5. Select air fry at 200°C for 10 minutes.
6. Flip the tofu slices over and brush with more olive oil.
7. Air fry for another 10 minutes.
8. Remove the tofu from the air fryer and drizzle with lime juice.
9. Season with salt and pepper to taste.
10. Garnish with fresh cilantro leaves and serve hot.

Thai-style tofu satay

Serves: 4

Prep time: 20 minutes / Cook time: 20 minutes

Ingredients:

- 1 block (400g) firm tofu, pressed and sliced into 1/2-inch thick pieces
- 60g creamy peanut butter

- 2 tbsp soy sauce
- 2 tbsp honey
- 1 lime, juiced
- 1 garlic clove, minced
- 1/2 tsp ground ginger
- Salt and pepper, to taste
- Fresh cilantro leaves, chopped peanuts, and lime wedges, for garnish

Instructions:

1. Preheat the air fryer to 200°C for 5 minutes.
2. In a bowl, whisk together the peanut butter, soy sauce, honey, lime juice, garlic, and ginger until smooth.
3. Coat each tofu slice in the peanut butter mixture.
4. Place the coated tofu slices on the crisper plate, making sure they are not touching each other.
5. Air fry the tofu at 200°C for 10 minutes, flipping halfway through the cooking time.
6. While the tofu is cooking, make the dipping sauce by combining the remaining peanut butter mixture with 2-3 tablespoons of water, until it reaches a dipping sauce consistency.
7. Once the tofu is done cooking, sprinkle it with salt and pepper to taste and garnish with chopped cilantro leaves and peanuts.
8. Serve with the dipping sauce and lime wedges on the side. Enjoy!

Lebanese-style falafel wraps

Serves: 4

Prep time: 30 minutes / Cook time: 12 minutes

Ingredients:

- For the falafel:
- 400g canned chickpeas, drained and rinsed
- 1 small onion, roughly chopped 2 garlic cloves, minced 2 tbsp fresh parsley, chopped
- 1 tbsp fresh coriander, chopped
- 1 tsp ground cumin
- 1/2 tsp ground coriander
- 1/4 tsp cayenne pepper
- Salt and pepper, to taste
- 60g plain flour 2 tbsp olive oil
- For the wraps:
- 4 wholemeal pitta breads

- 4 lettuce leaves, shredded
- 1 small red onion, thinly sliced
- 1 small cucumber, thinly sliced
- 4 tbsp hummus
- 4 tbsp tzatziki
- 4 lemon wedges, for serving

Instructions:

1. Preheat the air fryer to 180°C for 5 minutes.
2. In a food processor, pulse the chickpeas, onion, garlic, parsley, coriander, cumin, coriander, cayenne pepper, salt, and pepper until the mixture is coarse, but not pureed.
3. Add the flour and pulse again until the mixture comes together.
4. Shape the mixture into 16 small patties, about 2-3 cm in diameter.
5. Brush the patties with olive oil and place them on the crisper plate.
6. Select air fry at 180°C for 12 minutes.
7. When the falafel is cooked, remove it from the air fryer and set aside.
8. Warm the pitta breads in the air fryer for 1-2 minutes.
9. Stuff each pitta with lettuce, red onion, cucumber, 4 falafel patties, 1 tbsp of hummus and 1 tbsp of tzatziki.
10. Serve with a lemon wedge.

Italian-style warm caprese salad

Serves: 4

Prep time: 10 minutes / Cook time: 5 minutes

Ingredients:

- 4 large ripe tomatoes, sliced
- 1 ball (125g) fresh mozzarella cheese, sliced
- 10 fresh basil leaves, torn
- 2 tbsp extra-virgin olive oil
- 1 tbsp balsamic vinegar
- Salt and pepper, to taste

Instructions:

1. Arrange the sliced tomatoes and mozzarella cheese on a serving plate, alternating them.
2. Sprinkle the torn basil leaves over the top of the tomatoes and mozzarella.

3. Drizzle the olive oil and balsamic vinegar over the top of the salad.
4. Set the air fryer to 160 C and fry for 5 minutes or until the cheese is melting.
5. Season with salt and pepper, to taste.
6. Serve immediately.

Mexican-style black bean taquitos

Serves: 4

Prep time: 30 minutes / Cook time: 10 minutes

Ingredients:

- 1 can (400g) black beans, drained and rinsed
- 1 small onion, chopped
- 1 garlic clove, minced
- 1 tbsp olive oil
- 1/2 tsp ground cumin
- 1/2 tsp chilli powder
- 1/4 tsp paprika
- Salt and pepper, to taste
- 8 small flour tortillas
- 30g grated cheddar cheese
- Sour cream, salsa, and guacamole, for serving

Instructions:

1. Preheat the air fryer to 180°C for 5 minutes.
2. In a large frying pan, heat the olive oil over medium heat.
3. Add the onion and garlic and cook until the onion is soft, about 5 minutes.
4. Add the black beans, cumin, chilli powder, paprika, salt, and pepper.
5. Cook for another 5 minutes, stirring occasionally until the beans are heated through and the spices are fragrant.
6. Take off the heat and mash the black bean mixture with a fork or a potato masher until it forms a rough paste. Allow it to cool slightly.
7. Place a spoonful of the black bean mixture in the centre of each tortilla and sprinkle with grated cheddar cheese.
8. Roll up each tortilla tightly and place seam-side down on the crisper plate of the air fryer.
9. Spray the taquitos with cooking spray and air fry at 180°C for 10 minutes, or until golden brown and crispy.

10. Serve hot with sour cream, salsa, and guacamole on the side. Enjoy your delicious Mexican-style black bean taquitos!

Chinese-style vegetable dumplings

Serves: 4

Prep time: 30 minutes / Cook time: 10 minutes

Ingredients:

- For the dumpling dough:
- 300g plain flour
- 150ml hot water
- For the vegetable filling:
- 100g shiitake mushrooms, finely chopped
- 2 spring onions, finely chopped
- 1 garlic clove, minced
- 1 carrot, grated
- 1/4 head cabbage, finely shredded
- 1 tbsp soy sauce
- 1 tsp sesame oil
- 1 tsp grated ginger
- 1 tbsp cornflour
- Salt and pepper, to taste
- For the dipping sauce:
- 2 tbsp soy sauce
- 2 tbsp rice vinegar
- 1 tbsp honey
- 1 garlic clove, minced
- 1 tsp grated ginger
- 1 tsp sesame oil
- 1 tsp chilli flakes (optional)

Instructions:

1. In a large bowl, mix the flour with the hot water until a dough forms.
2. Knead for 5 minutes until smooth.
3. Cover and set aside for 20 minutes.
4. In a large frying pan, heat the sesame oil over medium heat.
5. Add the shiitake mushrooms, spring onions, and garlic and cook for 2-3 minutes until softened.
6. Add the grated carrot and cabbage, soy sauce, sesame oil, and grated ginger. Cook for 5 minutes until the vegetables are softened.

7. Stir in the cornflour to thicken the filling.
8. Season with salt and pepper to taste.
9. Roll the dough into a long cylinder and divide it into 24 pieces.
10. Roll each piece into a small ball and flatten with a rolling pin to create a small circle.
11. Place a small spoonful of the vegetable filling in the centre of each circle. Fold the dough over and seal the edges by pressing with your fingers or a fork.
12. Preheat the air fryer to 180°C for 5 minutes.
13. Place the dumplings in a single layer in the air fryer basket and spray with cooking oil.
14. Air fry for 10 minutes or until golden brown.
15. In a small bowl, mix the soy sauce, rice vinegar, honey, garlic, grated ginger, sesame oil, and chilli flakes (optional) to make the dipping sauce.
16. Serve the hot dumplings with the dipping sauce on the side.

Mediterranean-style stuffed artichokes

Serves: 4

Prep time: 20 minutes / Cook time: 30 minutes

Ingredients:

- 4 medium-sized artichokes
- Juice of 1 lemon
- 2 tbsp olive oil
- 1 onion, finely chopped
- 2 garlic cloves, minced
- 30g pine nuts
- 30g raisins
- 30g chopped fresh parsley
- 30g chopped fresh mint
- 30g breadcrumbs
- Salt and pepper, to taste

Instructions:

1. Cut off the top third of each artichoke and remove the outermost tough leaves. Using a spoon, remove the choke and any prickly inner leaves.
2. Rub the cut edges with lemon juice to prevent discoloration.
3. In a large frying pan, heat the olive oil over medium heat.

4. Add the onion and garlic and cook for 2-3 minutes until softened.
5. Add the pine nuts and raisins and cook for another 2-3 minutes until the pine nuts are lightly toasted.
6. Remove the pan from the heat and stir in the parsley, mint, breadcrumbs, salt, and pepper.
7. Spoon the filling into the artichoke cavities.
8. Preheat the air fryer to 180°C for 5 minutes.
9. Place the stuffed artichokes in a single layer in the air fryer basket and spray with cooking oil.
10. Air fry for 30 minutes or until the artichokes are tender and the filling is golden brown.
11. Serve the hot stuffed artichokes and enjoy!

Indian-style samosa chaat

Serves: 4

Prep time: 20 minutes / Cook time: 10 minutes

Ingredients:

- 4 samosas (store-bought or homemade)
- 1 can (400g) chickpeas, drained and rinsed
- 1 small onion, finely chopped
- 1 small tomato, finely chopped
- 1 green chilli, finely chopped
- 60g plain yoghurt
- 1 tbsp tamarind chutney
- 1 tsp chaat masala
- Salt, to taste
- Fresh coriander leaves, chopped for garnish
- Sev or crunchy fried noodles, for garnish

Instructions:

1. Preheat the air fryer to 180°C for 5 minutes.
2. Place the samosas on the crisper plate and spray them with a little oil.
3. Select air fry at 200°C and set the timer for 10 minutes.
4. While the samosas are cooking, in a large mixing bowl, add the chickpeas, onion, tomato, green chilli, yoghurt, tamarind chutney, chaat masala, and salt.
5. Mix well to combine.
6. Once the samosas are done, remove them from the air fryer and let them cool for a few minutes.
7. Cut them into bite-size pieces.

8. Add the samosa pieces to the mixing bowl with the chickpea mixture and toss to combine.
9. Transfer the samosa chaat to serving bowls, garnish with fresh coriander leaves and sev or crunchy fried noodles.
10. Serve immediately.

Italian-style stuffed mushrooms

Serves: 4

Prep time: 15 minutes / Cook time: 15 minutes

Ingredients:

- 8 large mushrooms
- 100g ricotta cheese
- 40g grated parmesan cheese
- 1 garlic clove, minced
- 1 tablespoon chopped fresh parsley
- 1 tablespoon chopped fresh basil
- 1 tablespoon olive oil
- Salt and black pepper, to taste

Instructions:

1. Preheat the air fryer to 180°C.
2. Clean the mushrooms with a damp paper towel and remove the stems.
3. In a bowl, combine ricotta cheese, parmesan cheese, garlic, parsley, basil, and salt and pepper.
4. Spoon the cheese mixture into each mushroom cap.
5. Drizzle the tops with olive oil.
6. Arrange the stuffed mushrooms in the air fryer basket and cook for 12-15 minutes, or until the mushrooms are tender and the cheese is melted and golden.

Korean-style tofu lettuce wraps

Serves: 4

Prep time: 20 minutes / Cook time: 10 minutes

Ingredients:

- 200g firm tofu, drained and crumbled
- 2 tablespoons soy sauce
- 1 tablespoon sesame oil
- 1 tablespoon honey

- 1 tablespoon rice vinegar
- 1 tablespoon gochujang (Korean hot pepper paste)
- 2 cloves garlic, minced
- 1 teaspoon grated ginger
- 1 tablespoon vegetable oil
- 1 head of butter lettuce, washed and separated into leaves
- 120g cooked rice
- 30g chopped scallions
- 30g chopped cilantro

Instructions:

1. In a bowl, whisk together soy sauce, sesame oil, honey, rice vinegar, gochujang, garlic, and ginger.
2. Preheat the air fryer to 180°C.
3. Drizzle vegetable oil into the air fryer basket.
4. Add crumbled tofu and fry for 3-4 minutes, or until browned.
5. Add the sauce mixture to the basket and stir to coat the tofu.
6. Air fry for 1-2 minutes, or until the sauce thickens slightly.
7. To assemble the lettuce wraps, spoon some rice onto each lettuce leaf, then top with the tofu mixture.
8. Sprinkle with scallions and cilantro, and serve immediately.

Middle Eastern-style stuffed grape leaves

Serves: 4

Prep time: 30 minutes / Cook time: 20 minutes

Ingredients:

- 1 jar of grape leaves (about 30 leaves)
- 200g ground lamb
- 1 onion, finely chopped
- 2 garlic cloves, minced
- 120g cooked rice
- 2 tablespoons chopped fresh mint
- 2 tablespoons chopped fresh parsley
- 1 tablespoon lemon juice
- 1/2 teaspoon ground cinnamon

- Salt and black pepper, to taste
- 30ml olive oil

Instructions:

1. Rinse the grape leaves under cold running water, then drain and pat dry.
2. Trim off the stems and discard.
3. Preheat the air fry to 180°C.
4. In a bowl, mix together ground lamb, onion, garlic, cooked rice, mint, parsley, lemon juice, cinnamon, salt, and pepper.
5. Place a grape leaf on a work surface, vein side up. Spoon 1 tablespoon of the lamb mixture in the centre of the leaf.
6. Fold the bottom of the leaf over the filling, then fold in the sides and roll up tightly.
7. Repeat with the remaining grape leaves and filling mixture.
8. Brush the bottom of the air fryer basket with olive oil.
9. Arrange the stuffed grape leaves in the basket, seam side down. Brush the tops with olive oil.
10. Air fry at 180°C for 20 minutes, or until the grape leaves are tender and lightly browned. Serve warm.

Lentil Soup

Serves 4

Prep time: 10 minutes / Cook time: 40 minutes

Ingredients:

- 1 tbsp olive oil
- 1 onion, diced
- 2 garlic cloves, minced
- 2 medium carrots, peeled and chopped
- 2 celery stalks, chopped
- 1 tsp ground cumin
- 1 tsp ground coriander
- 1 tsp smoked paprika
- 200g red lentils
- 1-litre vegetable stock
- 1 tbsp tomato paste
- Salt and pepper, to taste
- 2 tbsp chopped fresh parsley, for garnish (optional)

Instructions:

1. In a large pot, heat the olive oil over medium heat.
2. Add the onion and garlic and sauté until softened, about 3-4 minutes.
3. Add the carrots and celery and cook for another 5 minutes until slightly softened.
4. Add the cumin, coriander, and smoked paprika and cook for another minute.
5. Add the lentils, vegetable stock, and tomato paste. Bring to a boil and then reduce heat to low and simmer for 25-30 minutes, stirring occasionally, until the lentils are cooked through and the vegetables are soft.
6. Season with salt and pepper to taste.
7. If desired, sprinkle with chopped fresh parsley before serving.

20 Air Fryer Tofu Stir Fry with Vegetables

Serves 4

Prep time: 10 minutes / Cook time: 15-20 minutes

Ingredients:

- 450 g extra firm tofu, drained and cut into bite-sized cubes
- 2 tbsp cornstarch
- 1 tsp black pepper
- 2 bell peppers, sliced
- 2 cloves of garlic, minced
- 200 g broccoli florets
- 2 tbsp hoisin sauce
- 1 tsp salt
- 2 tbsp vegetable oil
- 1 onion, sliced
- 2 tbsp soy sauce
- 1 tsp sesame oil

Instructions:

1. In a large bowl, mix together the tofu, cornstarch, salt, and pepper until well coated.
2. Preheat the air fryer to 400°F (200°C).
3. Place the tofu in a single layer in the air fryer basket. Cook for 10-15 minutes, flipping the tofu halfway through cooking, or until crispy and golden brown. Remove from the air fryer and set aside.
4. In a large wok or frying pan, heat the vegetable oil over high heat. Add the bell peppers, onion, garlic, and broccoli, and stir-fry for 2-3 minutes or until the vegetables are tender.
5. Add the crispy tofu to the pan, along with the soy sauce, hoisin sauce, and sesame oil. Stir-fry for an additional 2-3 minutes or until the sauce is well combined and the tofu is heated through.
6. Serve hot over rice or noodles. Enjoy!

Tofu Wrap

Serves 4

Prep time: 5 minutes / Cook time: 15 minutes

Ingredients:

- 4 tortilla wraps
- 200g of pressed and cubed tofu
- 100g of soy sauce
- 100g of diced vegetables (such as peppers, onions, mushrooms)
- 2 tablespoons of sesame oil
- Salt and pepper, to taste

Instructions:

1. Preheat the air fryer to 180 °C.
2. In a mixing bowl, combine the cubed tofu, soy sauce, sesame oil, salt, and pepper. Mix until well combined.
3. Place the tofu and vegetable mixture in the air fryer and cook for 8-10 minutes or until the tofu is golden brown and crispy, flipping halfway through.
4. Remove from the air fryer and let it cool for a few minutes before serving.
5. Place the cooked tofu and vegetables in the centre of each tortilla wrap and roll them up tightly.
6. Place the wraps in the air fryer and cook for 2-3 minutes or until the tortilla is golden brown and crispy.

Vegan Roasted Vegetable Quinoa Bowl

Serves: 4

Prep time: 10 minutes / Cook time: 30 minutes

Ingredients:

- 1 cup quinoa, rinsed
- 2 cups water
- 2 cups chopped mixed vegetables (such as broccoli, bell pepper, zucchini, and onion)

- 2 tablespoons olive oil
- 1 teaspoon garlic powder Salt and pepper to taste
- 4 cups baby spinach leaves
- 1 avocado, sliced
- 2 tablespoons tahini
- 2 tablespoons lemon juice
- 1 tablespoon maple syrup
- 1/4 teaspoon salt
- 1/4 teaspoon
- Black pepper

Instructions:

1. Preheat the oven to 425°F (220°C). Line a baking sheet with parchment paper.
2. In a medium saucepan, bring the quinoa and water to a boil. Reduce heat to low, cover, and simmer for 15-20 minutes until the quinoa is cooked through.
3. In a large bowl, toss the mixed vegetables with olive oil, garlic powder, salt, and pepper. Spread the vegetables out onto the prepared baking sheet.
4. Roast in the preheated oven for 20-25 minutes until the vegetables are tender and lightly browned.
5. In a small bowl, whisk together the tahini, lemon juice, maple syrup, salt, and black pepper.
6. Divide the cooked quinoa, roasted vegetables, baby spinach, and avocado slices evenly among 4 bowls.
7. Drizzle each bowl with the tahini dressing and serve.

Salmon with Roasted Vegetables

Serves 4

Prep time: 15 minutes / Cook time: 30 minutes

Ingredients:

- 4 salmon fillets (approximately 170g each), skin on
- 1 red bell pepper, chopped
- 1 yellow bell pepper, chopped
- 1 zucchini, chopped
- 1 red onion, chopped
- 2 tablespoons olive oil

- Salt and pepper to taste
- 1 teaspoon dried thyme
- 1 teaspoon dried rosemary
- 1 teaspoon dried oregano

Preparation Instructions:

1. Preheat the oven to 200°C.
2. In a large bowl, mix together the chopped peppers, zucchini, and red onion with 2 tablespoons of olive oil. Add salt, pepper, thyme, rosemary, and oregano to taste, and stir to coat the vegetables evenly.
3. Spread the vegetables in a single layer on a baking sheet, and roast for 20-25 minutes, until they are tender and lightly browned.
4. Meanwhile, season the salmon fillets with salt and pepper on both sides. Place the fillets, skin side down, on a baking sheet lined with parchment paper.
5. Once the vegetables are done roasting, place the baking sheet with the salmon in the oven and roast for 10-12 minutes, until the salmon is cooked.
6. Serve the salmon fillets with roasted vegetables on the side, and enjoy!

Vegan Stuffed Bell Peppers

Serves 4

Prep time: 20 minutes / Cook time: 45 minutes

Ingredients:

- 4 bell peppers, halved and seeded
- 1 cup cooked brown rice
- 1 can black beans, drained and rinsed
- 1 small onion, diced
- 2 cloves garlic, minced
- 1 tablespoon olive oil
- 1 teaspoon ground cumin
- 1 teaspoon chilli powder
- Salt and pepper, to taste
- 1 cup tomato sauce
- 1 cup vegan shredded cheese

Instructions:

1. Preheat the oven to 375°F.
2. Heat the olive oil in a pan over medium heat.
3. dd the onion and garlic and sauté until tender. Add

the cooked rice, black beans, cumin, chili powder, salt, and pepper to the pan. Stir to combine.

4. Pour in the tomato sauce and stir to combine. Remove from heat. Place the bell pepper halves in a baking dish. Spoon the rice and bean mixture into the bell peppers.

5. Cover with foil and bake for 30 minutes. Remove the foil and sprinkle the vegan cheese on top.

6. Return to the oven and bake for an additional 10-15 minutes or until the cheese is melted and bubbly.

Air Fried Vegetable Fajitas with Guacamole

Serves 2

Prep time: 15 minutes / Cook time: 20 minutes

Ingredients

- 1 red bell pepper, sliced
- 1 green bell pepper, sliced
- 1 yellow onion, sliced
- 1 small zucchini, sliced
- 1 small yellow squash, sliced
- 1 tbsp olive oil
- 1 tsp chili powder
- 1 tsp ground cumin
- 1 tsp smoked paprika
- 1/2 tsp garlic powder
- 1/2 tsp onion powder
- Sea salt and ground black pepper, to taste
- 4 small tortillas
- Guacamole, for serving

Preparation Instructions

1. Preheat your air fryer to 200°C.

2. In a mixing bowl, combine sliced vegetables with olive oil, chili powder, cumin, smoked paprika, garlic powder, onion powder, sea salt, and black pepper. Mix well to coat.

3. Place the seasoned vegetables in the air fryer basket and cook for 15-20 minutes or until the

vegetables are tender and slightly charred.

4. Warm the tortillas in the microwave or on a skillet.

5. Assemble the fajitas by dividing the vegetables evenly among the tortillas.

6. Top each fajita with a spoonful of guacamole. Serve immediately and enjoy!

Air Fried Stuffed Portobello Mushrooms

Serves 4

Prep time: 15 minutes / Cook time: 15 minutes

Ingredients

- 4 large portobello mushrooms
- 1 tablespoon olive oil
- 1 small onion, diced
- 2 cloves garlic, minced
- 1/2 cup breadcrumbs
- 1/4 cup chopped fresh parsley
- 1/4 cup grated Parmesan cheese
- Salt and pepper to taste

Instructions

1. Preheat the air fryer to 350°F (175°C).

2. Remove the stems from the mushrooms and scoop out the gills with a spoon.

3. In a skillet, heat the olive oil over medium heat. Add the onion and garlic and cook until softened, about 3-4 minutes.

4. Add the breadcrumbs, parsley, Parmesan cheese, salt, and pepper to the skillet and stir until combined.

5. Stuff the mushroom caps with the breadcrumb mixture.

6. Place the stuffed mushrooms in the air fryer basket and cook for 10 minutes.

7. Flip the mushrooms and cook for another 5 minutes.

8. Serve hot.

Chapter 9: Desserts

Glazed donuts

Serves: 6 donuts

Prep time: 15 minutes / Cook time: 5 minutes

Ingredients

- 120 ml warm water
- 30 ml warm milk
- 1 tsp (3g) dry active yeast
- 35g granulated sugar + 13 g
- 28g unsalted butter, melted
- Half whole egg
- Half egg yolk
- ½ tsp (2ml) vanilla extract
- 160g all-purpose flour
- Small pinch of salt
- Cooking spray
- Glaze
- 120g powdered sugar
- 30 ml milk
- 7 ml golden syrup
- ¾ tsp (3ml) vanilla extract

Instructions

1. In a large measuring cup, add warm water, warm milk (45C), dry active yeast, and 13g of granulated sugar. Let the yeast mixture froth up and rise for about 5 minutes.
2. Now in a stand mixer, add the remaining of granulated sugar, unsalted melted butter, egg, egg yolk, vanilla extract, all-purpose flour (spooned and leveled off), and salt. Then pour in the yeast mixture and pace the hook attachment on and begin mixing on low speed until the flour is incorporated into liquids.
3. Next, increase the speed to high and beat for 5 minutes, and scrape down the sides of the beater bowl. If the dough looks too sticky, add 1 tablespoon of flour at a time. Make sure to mix well and scrape down the sides of the bowl between each addition of flour. (Don't add too much flour or the donuts will be too dry. They should have a slightly sticky texture to them).
4. Now place the dough in a large greased bowl and cover with a kitchen towel or plastic wrap. Let the dough rise for about one hour or until it doubles in size.
5. When the dough is ready, punch it down to release air bubbles and transfer it to a floured surface.
6. Using a rolling pin, roll the dough out to about 1.5 cm in thickness, and using a donut cutter cut out as many donuts as you can. Then reshape the scraps and cut out some more donuts.
7. Now place the cut-out donuts on a baking sheet lined with parchment paper then cover them lightly and let them rise again for about 20-30 minutes.
8. Preheat your air fryer to 175 C and spray the air fryer basket with cooking spray and place a few donuts into the air fryer basket and spray them with some more cooking spray. Make sure that the donuts are not touching.
9. Air-fry the donuts for about 4 minutes, and repeat this process with the remaining donuts and donut holes. Then transfer the donuts onto a plate lined with paper towels.
10. To make the glaze: In a large bowl combine sugar, milk, golden syrup, and vanilla extract. While the donuts are warm dip them in the glaze and let them set on a cooling rack. The glaze sets shinier when the donuts are hot. Enjoy!

Lava cake with vanilla ice cream

Serves: 3 cakes

Prep time: 10 minutes / Cook time: 3 minutes

Ingredients

- 75g milk chocolate chips
- 75g unsalted butter
- 1 egg
- A pinch of salt
- 40g plain flour
- Side
- Vanilla ice cream

Instructions

1. Place a bowl with the chocolate and butter on top of the hot water bath.
2. Stir as the heat melts the mixture until smooth consistency.
3. Remove the bowl from the fire.
4. Beat the egg in a small bowl and add it to the chocolate mixture. Stir well.
5. Add in salt and flour and stir well till smooth.
6. Add a coat of butter to your air fryer containers to aid easy removal of your cakes later, and add the mixture to your containers.
7. Preheat the air fryer to 160C for 5 mins and cook for about 2 to 3 mins.
8. Remove it from the air fryer once you see that the top is cooked and looks solid.
9. Remove from the air fryer, flip it over, add the vanilla ice cream on the side or top and enjoy!

Mini Peanut Butter Tarts

Serves 8

Prep time: 25 minutes / Cook time: 12-15 minutes

Ingredients

- 125 g pecans
- 110 g finely ground blanched almond flour
- 2 tablespoons unsalted butter, at room temperature
- 50 g powdered sweetener, plus 2 tablespoons, divided
- 120 g heavy (whipping) cream
- 2 tablespoons mascarpone cheese
- 110 g cream cheese
- 140 g sugar-free peanut butter
- 1 teaspoon pure vanilla extract
- ⅛ teaspoon sea salt
- 85 g organic chocolate chips
- 1 tablespoon coconut oil
- 40 g chopped peanuts or pecans

Instructions

1. Place the pecans in the bowl of a food processor; process until they are finely ground.
2. Transfer the ground pecans to a medium bowl and stir in the almond flour. Add the butter and

2 tablespoons of sweetener and stir until the mixture becomes wet and crumbly.
3. Divide the mixture among 8 silicone muffin cups, pressing the crust firmly with your fingers into the bottom and part way up the sides of each cup.
4. Arrange the muffin cups in the air fryer basket, working in batches if necessary. Set the air fryer to 148ºC and bake for 12 to 15 minutes, until the crusts begin to brown. Remove the cups from the air fryer and set them aside to cool.
5. In the bowl of a stand mixer, combine the heavy cream and mascarpone cheese. Beat until peaks form. Transfer to a large bowl.
6. In the same stand mixer bowl, combine the cream cheese, peanut butter, remaining 50 g sweetener, vanilla, and salt. Beat at medium-high speed until smooth. 7. Reduce the speed to low and add the heavy cream mixture back a spoonful at a time, beating after each addition.
7. Spoon the peanut butter mixture over the crusts and freeze the tarts for 30 minutes.
8. Place the chocolate chips and coconut oil in the top of a double boiler over high heat. Stir until melted, then remove from the heat.
9. Drizzle the melted chocolate over the peanut butter tarts. Top with the chopped nuts and freeze the tarts for another 15 minutes, until set.
10. Store the peanut butter tarts in an airtight container in the refrigerator for up to 1 week or in the freezer for up to 1 month.

Apple Pie

Serves 6

Prep time: 5 minutes / Cook time: 20 minutes

Ingredients

- Pre Made Pie crust x2
- 600g apple pie filling
- 1 tbsp unsalted butter
- 1 tsp white sugar
- 1 tsp cinnamon
- 1 tsp brown caster sugar

Instructions

1. Preheat the air fryer at 180°C for 4-5 minutes

2. Meanwhile, flatten the pie crusts if required
3. Place a crust on the pie pan,Evenly pour the apple filling from the can straight onto the pie crust
4. Add the second layer of crust over the apple pie
5. Trim and press down on the edges to seal the pie
6. Make 3 incisions on the centre of the pie using a bread knife. This ensures steam can be released during the cooking process
7. Brush the melted butter over the crust of the pie Sprinkle the sugar and cinnamon over the pie
8. Insert the pie in the air fryer and set the temperature to 210°C for 20-25 minutes
9. Retrieve the golden coloured pie and dust the caster sugar on top
10.Cut 6 slices for the family to enjoy as a dessert

Quiche Lorraine

Serves 4

Prep time: 20 minutes / Cook time: 40 minutes

.

Ingredients

- 1 sheet frozen puff pastry
- 30ml olive oil
- 175g boneless bacon strips
- 130g finely diced onion
- 5 large eggs
- 125ml double cream
- 125ml whole milk
- 100g grated Swiss-style
- ¼ tsp ground black pepper

Instructions

1. Preheat the air fryer at 180° for 5 minutes
2. Meanwhile, line a 4"x18" tart tin with puff pastry (detachable base tin).Layer the pastry with baking paper
3. Place the tin in the air fryer and cook for 7 minutes at 180°C
4. Remove the baking paper.Make light incisions in the paste with a fork
5. Return to air fryer to cook for another 5-6 minutes, then set the pastry aside
6. Place a large pan on a medium heated stove and add oil and bacon for 4-5 minutes
7. Toss in the onions and continue cooking for another 4-5 minutes
8. Once the food content is crisp and golden, set aside
9. Using a stand mixer, whisk eggs, cream, milk, and black pepper
10.Scrape the into the base of the pastry. Dash cheese on top of the pastry
11.Pour the creamy egg content on top of the cheese
12.Place the food content back into the air fryer at 160°C for 30 minutes
13.Retrieve the Quiche and set aside to cool . Cut into 4 quarters, or 6 pieces if you have a larger family

Rich chocolatey custard

Serves 2

Prep time: 15 minutes / Cook time: 10 minutes

Ingredients

- 180 g whipping cream
- 2 egg yolks
- 50 g caster sugar
- 65 g dark chocolate
- ⅛ teaspoon salt
- ⅛ teaspoon vanilla extract

Instructions

1. Whisk sugar, egg yolks, salt and vanilla in a mixing bowl.
2. Chop dark chocolate into chip sized pieces.
3. Bring the cream to a low simmer over a medium heat for 3-4 minutes.
4. Slowly, add egg yolk mix to the cream, constantly stirring to combine.
5. Add the chocolate to the pan and continue to heat until chocolate has melted.
6. Preheat the air fryer for 2 minutes.
7. Pour the chocolate mix into two ramekins.
8. Put the ramekins in the pre heated air fryer and cook for 7 minutes.
9. Allow custard to cool on a wire rack for 20 minutes.
10.Cool custard in fridge.

Chocolate Cheesecake

Serves 8

Prep time: 10 minutes / Cook time: 20 minutes

Ingredients

- 230 g cream cheese
- 45 g soft butter
- 100 g crushed digestive biscuits
- 2 eggs
- 75 g sugar
- 200 g melted chocolate
- 1 teaspoon vanilla extract
- 1 tablespoon flour

Instructions:

1. Melt the butter over a low heat.
2. Once melted, add the biscuit crumbs and mix well.
3. Press the buttered biscuit crumb into the bottom of a springform tin.
4. Set in fridge / freezer while preparing the rest of the recipe.
5. In a mixing bowl, mix cream cheese and sugar. Beat in eggs one at a time.
6. Add flour and vanilla extract to the filling mixture.
7. Slowly pour melted chocolate into the filling mixture.
8. Stirring all the time to evenly distribute the chocolate.
9. Spoon filling over biscuit base.
10. Bake for 15 - 20 minutes in an air fryer at 220°C.
11. Cool and refrigerate until cheesecake is fully set.

Air fryer Olives

Serves 2

Prep time: 5minutes / Cook time: 10-12 minutes

Ingredients:

- 20 g plain flour
- 30 g panko bread crumbs
- 1 egg
- 15 g grated parmesan cheese
- 120 g olives

Instructions:

1. Mix parmesan and bread crumbs together.
2. Prepare a coating station with three bowls - egg in one bowl, flour in another and parmesan bread crumbs in the third bowl.
3. Bread olives by placing them in flour first,then egg and finally breadcrumbs.
4. Air fry at 200°C for 10 - 12 minutes.

Grilled Air Fryer Peaches:

Serves 2

Prep time: 5minutes / Cook time: 14 minutes

Ingredients:

- Fresh peaches 4
- 2 tsp butter
- Peach cobbler
- 1 tbsp honey
- 1 tsp ground ginger

Instructions:

1. Slice the peaches and put them in air fryer basket.
2. Spray the sliced peaches with extra virgin oil.
3. Air fryer the peaches at 200 degrees Celsius or 400 degrees Fahrenheit for 8 minutes.
4. Place peach cobbler topping in a bowl and break it until it gains texture like breadcrumbs.
5. Remove the sliced peaches from air fryer and place them on a foil.
6. Now sprinkle the peaches with ginger and drizzle them with honey.
7. Now add butter and cobbler topping on peaches.
8. Place them back into air fryer at 200 degrees Celsius or 400 degrees Fahrenheit for 6 minutes.
9. On beeping, remove grilled peaches from air fryer and serve them with cream.

10 Air fryer Banana Souffle

Serves 4

Prep time: 3minutes / Cook time: 15 minutes

Ingredients:

- 2 medium sized bananas

- Extra virgin oil for spraying
- 2 large eggs
- ½ tsp cinnamon

Instructions:

1. Peel the bananas and add them to blender. Add eggs to them.
2. Add cinnamon to the blender and pulse until it gets smooth.
3. Use extra virgin oil to spray ramekins.
4. Put soufflé better into ramekins and place them in air fryer.
5. Air fryer the batter at 180 degrees Celsius or 360 degrees Fahrenheit for 15 minutes.
6. Serve the soufflés quickly before they start to fall.

Mixed Berries with Pecan Streusel Topping

Serves 3

Prep time: 5minutes / Cook time: 17 minutes

Ingredients:

- 75 g mixed berries
- Cooking spray

Topping:

- 1 egg, beaten
- 3 tablespoons almonds, slivered
- 3 tablespoons chopped pecans
- 2 tablespoons chopped walnuts
- 3 tablespoons granulated sweetener
- 2 tablespoons cold salted butter, cut into pieces
- ½ teaspoon ground cinnamon

Instructions:

1. Preheat the air fryer to 172°C. Lightly spray a baking dish with cooking spray.
2. Make the topping: In a medium bowl, stir together the beaten egg, nuts, sweetener, butter, and cinnamon until well blended.
3. Put the mixed berries in the bottom of the baking dish and spread the topping over the top.
4. Bake in the preheated air fryer for 17 minutes, or until the fruit is bubbly and topping is golden brown.
5. Allow to cool for 5 to 10 minutes before serving.

Pumpkin Pudding with Vanilla Wafers

Serves 4

Prep time: 10 minutes / Cook time: 12-17 minutes

Ingredients

- 250 g canned no-salt-added pumpkin purée (not pumpkin pie filling)
- 50 g packed brown sugar
- 3 tablespoons plain flour
- 1 egg, whisked
- 2 tablespoons milk
- 1 tablespoon unsalted butter, melted
- 1 teaspoon pure vanilla extract
- 4 low-fat vanilla, or plain wafers, crumbled
- Nonstick cooking spray

Instructions:

1. Preheat the air fryer to 176°C. Coat a baking pan with nonstick cooking spray. Set aside.
2. Mix the pumpkin purée, brown sugar, flour, whisked egg, milk, melted butter, and vanilla in a medium bowl and whisk to combine. Transfer the mixture to the baking pan.
3. Place the baking pan in the air fryer basket and bake for 12 to 17 minutes until set.
4. Remove the pudding from the basket to a wire rack to cool.
5. Divide the pudding into four bowls and serve with the vanilla wafers sprinkled on top.

Blackberry Peach Cobbler with Vanilla

Serves 4

Prep time: 10 minutes / Cook time: 20 minutes

Ingredients

Filling:

- 170 g blackberries
- 250 g chopped peaches, cut into ½-inch thick slices
- 2 teaspoons arrowroot or cornflour
- 2 tablespoons coconut sugar

- 1 teaspoon lemon juice

- 2 tablespoons sunflower oil
- 1 tablespoon maple syrup
- 1 teaspoon vanilla
- 3 tablespoons coconut sugar
- 40 g rolled oats
- 45 g whole-wheat pastry, or plain flour
- 1 teaspoon cinnamon
- ¼ teaspoon nutmeg
- ⅛ teaspoon sea salt

Instructions:

1. Make the Filling: 1. Combine the blackberries, peaches, arrowroot, coconut sugar, and lemon juice in a baking pan.
2. Using a rubber spatula, stir until well incorporated. Set aside. Make the Topping:
3. Preheat the air fryer to 162°C
4. Combine the oil, maple syrup, and vanilla in a mixing bowl and stir well. Whisk in the remaining Ingredients. Spread this mixture evenly over the filling.
5. Place the pan in the air fryer basket and bake for 20 minutes, or until the topping is crispy and golden brown. Serve warm

Air fryer Yorkshire pudding

Serves 4

Prep time: 5 minutes / Cook time: 15 minutes

Ingredients

- Yorkshire pudding tin
- Salt and pepper to taste
- 1 tbsp extra virgin oil
- 1 small egg
- 150ml whole milk
- 50 g plain flour r

Instructions:

1. Set your Air Fryer to a temperature of 200 degrees Celsius (400 degrees Fahrenheit).
2. In a bowl, combine the plain flour with the flavor and mix well. While gently whisking with a fork, pour in the egg. Continue doing so until all of the egg has been incorporated.

3. The milk should be added in small increments while the mixture is being stirred frequently until it reaches the consistency of a thick batter.
4. To ensure that bubbles develop on the surface, give it a thorough beating.
5. Put a little olive oil in each of the Yorkshire pudding tins, then put them in the Air Fryer and cook them for five minutes, or until the oil starts to smoke.
6. Place the Yorkshire pudding tin back into the Air Fryer and pour in your Ingredients so that it reaches halfway up the tin. Cook at 200 degrees Celsius for 15 minutes

Air fryer Apple fries

Serves 4

Prep time: 5 minutes / Cook time: 15 minutes

Ingredients

- 6 apples of medium size
- 1 tbsp cinnamon
- 1 tbsp extra virgin avocado oil

Instructions:

1. Thinly slice the medium sized apples using mandolin or some other thing similar to it.
2. Toss the sliced apples in extra virgin avocado oil or preferred healthy oil.
3. Sprinkle the apples in cinnamon.
4. Place the sliced apples in air fryer at temperature of 200 degrees Celsius or 400 degrees Fahrenheit and cook them for 15 minutes.
5. Serve apple fries with seasoning of your choice.

Air Fryer Coconut Shrimp with Sweet Chilli Sauce

Serves 4

Prep time: 10 minutes / Cook time: 8-10 minutes

Ingredients

- 500 g large raw shrimp, peeled and deveined
- 113g unsweetened coconut flakes
- 113g Panko breadcrumbs

- 28g cornstarch
- 5g salt
- 2 eggs, beaten
- Sweet chilli sauce

Instructions:

1. Rinse and pat dry the shrimp.
2. In a shallow dish, mix together the coconut flakes, Panko breadcrumbs, cornstarch and salt.
3. In another shallow dish, beat the eggs.
4. Dip each shrimp in the beaten eggs, then coat in the coconut mixture.
5. Place the coated shrimp in a single layer in the air fryer basket.
6. Cook at 200°C (400°F) for 8-10 minutes or until the shrimp are golden brown and cooked through.
7. Serve the cooked shrimp with sweet chilli sauce for dipping.
8. Enjoy your delicious and crispy Air Fryer Coconut Shrimp with Sweet Chilli Sauce!

Air Fryer Carrot Fries with Honey Mustard Dip

Serves 4

Prep time:10 minutes / Cook time: 15-20 minutes

Ingredients

- 500 g Carrots, peeled and cut into sticks
- 1 tbsp Olive Oil
- Salt, to taste
- Black Pepper, to taste
- 1 tsp Paprika

For the Honey Mustard Dip:

- 150 g Mayonnaise
- 2 tbsp Dijon Mustard
- 2 tbsp Honey
- Salt, to taste
- Black Pepper, to taste

Instructions:

1. Preheat the air fryer to 180°C.
2. In a bowl, mix the carrots with the olive oil, salt, pepper, and paprika.
3. Place the carrots in the air fryer basket in a single layer and cook for 15-20 minutes, flipping them

halfway through.
4. While the carrots are cooking, prepare the honey mustard dip. In a small bowl, whisk together the mayonnaise, Dijon mustard, honey, salt, and pepper.
5. Serve the cooked carrots with the honey mustard dip on the side. Enjoy!

Grilled Pineapple Dessert

Serves 4

Prep time:5 minutes / Cook time: 12 minutes

Ingredients

- Coconut, or avocado oil for misting, or cooking spray
- 4½-inch-thick slices fresh pineapple, core removed
- 1 tablespoon honey
- ¼ teaspoon brandy, or apple juice
- 2 tablespoons slivered almonds, toasted
- Vanilla frozen yogurt, coconut sorbet, or ice cream

Instructions:

1. Spray both sides of pineapple slices with oil or cooking spray. Place into air fryer basket.
2. Air fry at 200ºC for 6 minutes. Turn slices over and cook for an additional 6 minutes.
3. Mix together the honey and brandy.
4. Remove cooked pineapple slices from air fryer, sprinkle with toasted almonds, and drizzle with honey mixture.
5. Serve with a scoop of frozen yogurt or sorbet on the side.

Printed in Great Britain
by Amazon

21055596R00054